CHARLIE BROWN'S
CYCLOPEDIA

HOW MACHINES WORK
Gears, Gizmos, and Gadgets

VOLUME · 6 ·

Based on the Charles M. Schulz Characters
Funk & Wagnalls

Charlie Brown's 'Cyclopedia
has been produced
by Mega-Books of New York,
Inc. in conjunction
with the editorial, design,
and marketing staff of
Field Publications.

STAFF FOR MEGA-BOOKS

Pat Fortunato
Editorial Director

Diana Papasergiou
Production Director

Susan Lurie
Executive Editor

Rosalind Noonan
Senior Editor

Adam Schmetterer
Research Director

**Michaelis/Carpelis
Design Assoc., Inc.**
Art Direction and Design

STAFF FOR FIELD PUBLICATIONS

Cathryn Clark Girard
Assistant Vice President,
Juvenile Publishing

Elizabeth Isele
Executive Editor

Kristina Jones
Executive Art Director

Leslie Erskine
Marketing Manager

Elizabeth Zuraw
Senior Editor

Michele Italiano-Perla
Group Art Director

Kathleen Hughes
Senior Art Director

Photograph and Illustration Credits:
Brent Bear/West Light, 22; The Bettmann Archive, 48, 49, 50; Richard Fukuhara/West Light, 17; Gary Gladstone/Image Bank, 54; Peter Grumman/Image Bank, 56; Gregory Heisler/Image Bank, 57; Walter Hodges/West Light, 21; Nick Nicholson/Image Bank, 34; Chuck O'Rear/West Light, 47, 52; Robert Phillips/Image Bank, 36; Mary Ellen Senor, 15, 16, 20, 21, 23, 26, 30, 34, 36, 37, 43, 50, 57; Courtesy Shimano, 32; Hans Wendler /Image Bank, 28; Eric L. Wheater/Image Bank, 36, 41.

ISBN: 0-8374-0051-1

Part of the material in this volume was previously published in *Charlie Brown's Second Super Book of Questions and Answers*.

Funk & Wagnalls, founded in 1876, is the publisher of *Funk & Wagnalls New Encyclopedia*, one of the most widely owned home and school reference sets, and many other adult and juvenile educational publications.

INTRODUCTION

Welcome to volume 6 of *Charlie Brown's 'Cyclopedia!* Have you ever wondered how a toaster knows when to pop up, or where escalator steps go after they disappear, or who invented the zipper? Charlie Brown and the rest of the *Peanuts* gang are here to help you find the answers to these questions and many more about how machines work. Have fun!

CONTENTS

WHEELS AND AXLES: DOORKNOB, ROLLER SKATES.

CHAPTER 1

MACHINES INSIDE OUT

Machines come in all sizes. They can be as big as a house or small enough to fit in the palm of your hand. They may be made of many parts, or they may be very simple, but all machines are used to do special jobs. Let's see what machines are made of and how they do their work!

THE MARVELS OF MACHINES

What is a machine?

A machine is an object that makes hard work easier or slow work faster. It gives the person using it greater speed or greater force. *Force* means a push or pull. A machine is usually made up of a few connected parts. A vacuum cleaner is a machine that makes housecleaning easier. A car is a machine that lets people move much faster than they could by walking. A telephone is a machine that makes talking to someone far away possible.

What are machines made of?

Machines can be simple or complex. Simple machines are made up of only one part. Complex machines have many parts. No matter how complicated the machine, if you take it apart, you end up with a combination of simple machines. There are six types of simple machines:

1. the lever
2. the inclined plane
3. the wedge
4. the screw
5. the wheel and axle
6. the pulley

Things such as gears, cranks, and springs are based on these simple machines.

Do all machines have motors?

No. There are many machines that do not have motors. The power for doing work with many of these machines comes from people's muscles. A broom is a kind of machine that needs your muscles. If you're sweeping the floor, you need your muscles to do the pushing—though the broom makes the sweeping job easier. Scissors, a shovel, a bottle opener, and a seesaw are also examples of motorless machines that need your muscles to help do the work.

LEVERS: SEESAW, TWEEZERS CHOPSTICKS, BOTTLE OPENER, FISHING ROD AND REEL, PIANO.

WHEELS AND AXLES: DOORKNOB, ROLLER SKATES.

What machines will we meet?

Here are some examples of the machines you and your family probably use every day. So come along with the *Peanuts* gang, and they'll show you how machines work.

Machines are very old! Back in the fifteenth century, the Italian artist and inventor Leonardo da Vinci filled notebooks with drawings of simple and complicated machines!

SCREWS: FAUCET, CORKSCREW.

WEDGES: ZIPPER, SAW, KNIFE, NEEDLE, LAWN MOWER, ELECTRIC SHAVER.

SPRINGS: POGO STICK, DIVING BOARD, BOW AND ARROW, MUSIC BOX, TOASTER, STAPLER, WIND UP CLOCK, BATHROOM SCALE.

INCLINED PLANE: LOADING PLATFORM.

PULLEYS: VENETIAN BLINDS, ELEVATOR

GEARS: ALARM CLOCK, BICYCLE, ESCALATOR.

ROLLER COASTER, STEERING WHEEL.

CRANKS: EGG BEATER, HAND DRILL, PENCIL SHARPENER.

PEANUTS

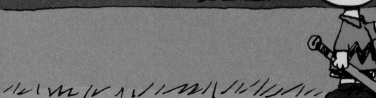

Even though levers aren't fancy or complicated, you couldn't get by without them. You use them to pry and balance things—even to play! As you look around, you'll be surprised at how much they can help you do.

LEAVE IT TO LEVERS

LEVERS IN OUR EVERYDAY LIVES

What is a lever?

A lever (LEV-ur) is a stiff bar that turns on a point. This point is called a fulcrum (FULL-crum). The seesaw on your playground is an example of a kind of machine called a lever. When a seesaw is used by two people who weigh about the same, its fulcrum is right around the center of the bar.

With a seesaw, you can lift a person heavier than you are if the heavier person moves forward on the seesaw, closer to the fulcrum. You certainly couldn't do that without the help of a machine!

WEIGHT OF SNOOPY

WEIGHT OF EIGHT BIRDS

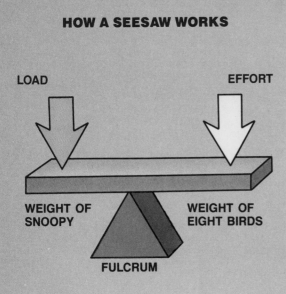

HOW A SEESAW WORKS

LOAD

EFFORT

WEIGHT OF SNOOPY

WEIGHT OF EIGHT BIRDS

FULCRUM

You can lift a load with a fulcrum and an equal amount of effort. The force you use is called effort.

Two high school students in Auburn, Washington, kept seesawing for 1,101 hours and 40 minutes!

What lever helps open bottles?

Some bottles do not have caps that are screwed on. With these bottles, it is nearly impossible to pull the cap off by hand. By using a bottle opener, another example of a lever, a bottle cap can be lifted off easily. One end of the lever is attached to the bottle. When your hand applies a small force to the other end of the lever, the cap lifts right off.

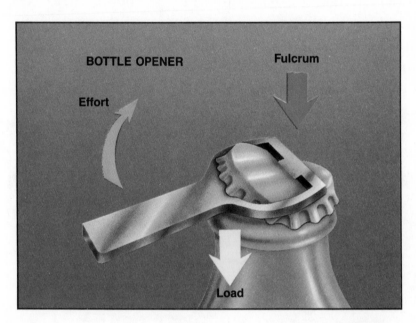

BOTTLE OPENER

Fulcrum

Effort

Load

How do levers help a piano make music?

The keys of a piano are attached to levers. When Schroeder pushes a piano key, a hammer at the end of a lever strikes wires inside the piano. This action creates a sound.

What lever helps take a splinter out of your skin?

A pair of tweezers is a lever that you can use to lift a splinter out of your skin. A small movement of your fingers against the two sides of the lever creates a larger movement in the tweezers, and lifts out the splinter.

Chopsticks are helpful levers—
especially when you're hungry!

Can people use levers to eat with?

Many people around the world do just that. They eat with levers called chopsticks. Like tweezers, a small movement of the fingers against the chopsticks creates a larger movement to help pick up the food.

Chopsticks were first used in China. The name comes from the Chinese word *K'wai-tsze* (kwhy-tzoo), which means "quick ones." Made of bamboo, wood, plastic, ivory, or metal, chopsticks are now used all over the world.

Why do people use a rod and reel for fishing?

People use a rod and reel to get their bait into deep water, where the big fish are. When you fish from the edge of a lake or river, or from an ocean beach, you are far from the deep water. The fishing rod is a lever that helps you throw your fishing line farther than your arm could do alone. You also need a very long line. The reel is used to store the line neatly and keep it from getting tangled.

When the line is thrown—or cast, as fishermen say— the reel lets the line go out very far. The hand that is placed on the reel closer to the body acts as the fulcrum, the turning point, while the other hand supplies the effort.

Have you ever tried to pull a wagon? What would happen if you had to pull it up a long flight of steps? Impossible? Well, you could try lifting the wagon, but that would be too heavy a job. No, that's not the answer at all. What you need is a ramp, one type of inclined plane that tackles tough tasks. Other variations of inclined planes—the wedge and the screw—also help to get many jobs done.

THE INCREDIBLE INCLINED PLANE

INCLINED PLANES

What is an inclined plane?

An inclined plane is a tilted, flat surface. It makes moving things between high and low places easier.

How do we use inclined planes?

An inclined plane can be used to load heavy boxes into a truck. Most people are not strong enough to lift such boxes, but placing a ten-foot plank with one end in the truck and the other end on the ground makes this task easy to do! Often this machine has little rollers on it. The rollers help the boxes slide easily up the tilted plane.

Such inclined planes, or ramps, were also used in Egypt back in 2600 B.C. to build huge pyramids and temples. These long, tilted ramps allowed workers to move very heavy stone blocks to the tops of pyramids and temples.

Airplanes got their name from the planes, or flat surfaces, that hold them up in the air. These flat surfaces are the wings!

WEDGES

What is a wedge?

A wedge is a special type of inclined plane. It has two or more surfaces that slope to an edge or a point. A log splitter is a kind of wedge. First the wedge is placed on the end of a log. When someone strikes the wedge with a mallet or hammer, the wedge is forced into the log. The sides of the wedge push the log apart. The wedge changes the downward force of the hammer into a sideward force that pushes the log apart. The deeper the wedge goes in, the more the two halves of the log are pushed apart. Finally, the log splits into two pieces.

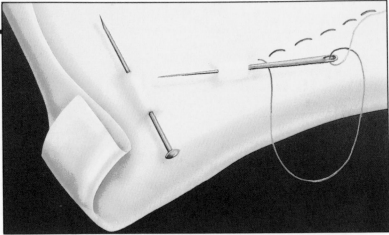

Pins and needles are two examples of wedges used on clothes.

What are some other machines that use a wedge?

Almost all machines that cut use a wedge. Axes, hatchets, and knives are sharp tools that are shaped like wedges to help them work better. Pins, needles, and nails are examples of pointed wedges. The points help the pin, needle, or nail go in easier. The material that is in the way is pushed to the side to let the pin, needle, or nail go through.

For example, a flat-ended pin would push the material ahead of it, instead of to the side. It would be very hard to make this kind of pin go through any material.

This man needs a saw with a nine-foot blade for a big task.

Some saws have teeth made of diamonds!

How does a saw work?

A saw works like hundreds of very tiny axes chopping. Each tooth on a saw blade is like a tiny, sharp ax. When you make a saw go back and forth across what you are cutting, the teeth bite off little chunks. Each little chunk is a piece of sawdust. Axes or hatchets, on the other hand, strike with a much greater force. They bite big chunks out of a piece of wood. For that reason, a saw is used for making careful, neat cuts in wood, plastic, or metal. An ax or a hatchet is used to make big, deep cuts.

Why do sharp knives cut better than dull knives?

In order to cut through something tough, such as the skin of a tomato, you need a special wedge—a knife—but its blade needs to be sharp. The reason is that sharp knife blades are thinner than dull knife blades, and sharp blades also have a rougher edge than dull ones. There are tiny teeth, so small you can see them only under a microscope, all along that rough edge of a sharp blade. If it's the blade of a steak knife, however, then it has large teeth. These teeth bite and tear at the tomato skin. Because a sharp blade is very thin, it has a very narrow area of tomato skin to push through. A dull blade is wider than a sharp blade, so it has to push through more tomato skin. A dull blade can cut only soft things, such as butter.

21

How do artists use wedges?

Artists who make wooden statues sometimes use a wedge called a chisel. They place the chisel against a wooden block, then bang on it with a mallet. Pieces of the wood block are cut off, and a beautiful sculpture is created.

With a simple wedge, this artist can bring a block of wood to life.

How does a lawn mower cut grass?

Lawn mowers use wedges called blades. The most popular type of lawn mower is the rotary power mower. *Rotary* means turning or spinning around. A rotary blade spins like a fan or an airplane propeller. A gasoline or electric motor supplies the energy to spin the blade. When the blade spins, it creates a wind underneath the mower. This moving air makes the blades of grass stand up straight. Then the mower chops them all off at the same height. The result is a lawn that looks smooth and even.

I HATE LAWN MOWERS!

The biggest lawn mower on record is 60 feet wide. It can mow one acre of grass in one minute!

What kind of power wedge can you find in the bathroom?

Electric shavers use wedges to cut hair, but they also need to protect the skin from getting cut. Most electric shavers have a metal screen that glides over the skin but also allows the hairs into the shaver. The screen holds the hairs in place as the cutting blades—small, sharp wedges—spin around and slice off the hairs.

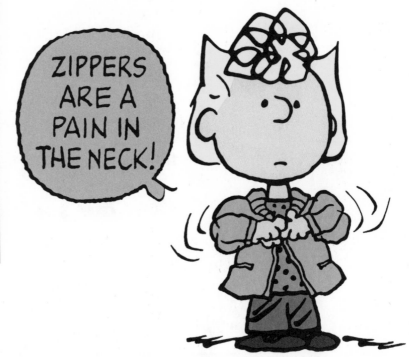

ELECTRIC SHAVER

CIRCLE OF BLADES

BLADE SCREEN

There's probably a power wedge in your very own home.

ZIPPERS ARE A PAIN IN THE NECK!

What makes a zipper work?

A zipper works because of wedges! If you look at a zipper, you'll see two rows of teeth that lock together when you zip it up. A little bump on the top of each tooth fits into a little hole in the bottom of the tooth above it. The part that you pull up and down is called the slide. The slide contains wedges that magnify the small effort that you use to open or close the zipper.

Inside the slide is a Y-shaped track surrounded by three wedges. When you open the zipper, the rows of teeth run through this track and the upper wedge forces the teeth apart. When you close the zipper, two lower wedges force the teeth back together, making them mesh and lock.

On some zippers, the teeth are made of metal. Other zippers have plastic teeth, and each row of teeth looks like a long, thin spring or spiral.

SCREWS

Is a screw a machine?

Yes. Screws are really inclined planes in spiral form. When you turn a screw, its spiral threads, or ridges, turn to make the small force of your muscles into a larger force. This force helps drive a screw into wood or other objects.

How does a corkscrew work?

A corkscrew is a spiral, pointed piece of metal that is used to remove corks from bottles. One end of the corkscrew is attached to a handle. The other end—the sharp end—is placed in the center of the cork. As the handle is turned, the corkscrew is driven into the cork. Once the corkscrew is inside the cork, a strong pull will remove the cork from the neck of the bottle.

How does a faucet work?

A faucet is attached to the end of a water pipe. The faucet holds the water in the pipe until you decide to let some out.

There is a hole between the water pipe and the spigot, the part of the faucet from which water flows. Inside the faucet is a screw that drives a plug into the hole. When you don't want water to come out, you want the hole to be plugged up. When you want water, you want the hole to be open. Turning the handle in one direction causes the plug to come out of the hole. Then water flows through. Turning the handle in the other direction puts the plug back in the hole. Then water can't leave the pipe.

The ancient Romans were using water faucets about 2,000 years ago!

CHAPTER 4

ROUND AND ROUND, UP AND DOWN

Machines that roll have them . . . so do machines that spin round and round. What makes these things turn? Wheels and axles! It's a very simple idea that does some amazing things—especially when wheels are used with ropes to make pulleys.

LET'S TAKE A SPIN WITH WHEELS

SO HERE I AM RIDING ON THE BACK OF MOM'S BICYCLE...

NOW IT'S A SHOPPING CART IN THE SUPERMARKET...

NOW IT'S A STROLLER THROUGH THE MALL...THEN, BACK ON THE BICYCLE...

SOMETIMES I GO A WHOLE DAY WITHOUT EVER TOUCHING THE GROUND!

How are wheels used?

Wheels help people and things move more easily. Cars and trains could not work if they didn't have wheels on which to move. Neither could bicycles, skateboards, roller skates, shopping carts, baby carriages, and many other things. Wheels sometimes connect motors to machines. In this way, motors rather than people can supply the energy to make the machines work.

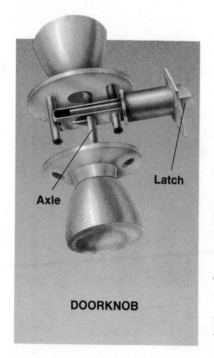

Latch

Axle

DOORKNOB

How does a doorknob work?

A doorknob is a wheel attached to a rod called an axle. The axle goes through the door. At the other end of the axle is another doorknob. When you turn one of the doorknobs, it turns the axle. The axle pushes a bar that's connected to the latch. The latch is the piece of metal that sticks out of the edge of the door. It fits into a little hole in the wall when the door is closed. The latch keeps the door from opening until you turn the knob. When you close the door, a spring makes the latch pop into the hole in the wall. The same spring also makes the doorknob turn back into place after you let go. You'll learn more about springs in chapter 5.

What makes roller skates and skateboards roll easily?

Inside the wheels of roller skates and skateboards are little steel balls called ball bearings. The ball bearings fit into grooves between the wheels and the axles. If there were no ball bearings, the wheels would rub and scrape on the axles. This kind of rubbing and scraping is called friction (FRICK-shun). It makes wheels hard to turn. If wheels are hard to turn, they can't roll fast. Ball bearings reduce friction and make wheels easy to turn. You can reduce friction even more if you squirt a drop of oil on the ball bearings. Bicycles, cars, and many other kinds of machines use ball bearings and oil or grease to make them run better.

The highest speed recorded on a skateboard is 71.79 mph in California by Richard Brown on June 17, 1979!

27

How did factories make their machines run before engines and motors were developed?

They used water wheels. This meant that factories had to be built close to a fast-flowing stream or river. A water wheel was made of wood. It had paddles or buckets around the rim. Part of the wheel was always in the water. As the stream flowed, water pushed against the paddles or buckets. It made the wheel turn. The wheel was attached to an axle called a drive shaft. Drive shafts were often very large. Some were made from the whole trunk of a tall tree. The drive shaft reached from the water wheel to the inside of the factory. When the water wheel turned, it made the drive shaft run the machines. In many factories, the drive shaft was used to turn other drive shafts. In that way, many machines could run at the same time.

PULLEYS ALL AROUND US

What is a pulley?

A pulley is a wheel that has a groove in the rim to hold a rope or cord. The groove in the wheel holds a rope and keeps it from slipping off. If you hang a pulley from a high place, like a ceiling or a tree limb, you can use it to lift a heavy object easily.

With a pulley, you are not using just your muscles to lift. You are also using the weight of your body. As long as the object you are lifting weighs less than you, you can lift it with a single pulley just by attaching it to one end of the rope and pulling down on the other end.

With the help of two double pulleys, you can lift a weight that's four times heavier than you!

What makes an elevator work?

With the help of pulleys, elevators lift and lower people from one floor to another. When you step into an elevator and push the button, an electric motor starts up. The motor is in a room at the top of the building. The motor pulls a set of cables that lifts the box in which you are riding. This box is called the elevator car. Each cable is a rope made of wires twisted or woven together. The cables run over pulleys attached to the motor. The end of the cables not attached to the car go down the elevator shaft to a counterweight. A counterweight is a weight that balances the car. When the car goes up, the counterweight goes down. When the car goes down, the counterweight goes up. An elevator has an automatic brake that stops the car if it begins to fall.

How do venetian blinds open and close?

Inside the venetian blinds, there's a pulley that makes them open and close. When you pull on a cord, it sets off a chain of events. The cord turns a pulley. The pulley turns a screw. The screw turns a gear. (You'll learn more about gears in chapter 5.) The turning gear then changes the slant of the top strip, or slat. This changes the slant of all the slats in the blind. As the slats move into a horizontal position, more light can come in. Horizontal means that the flat part of the slat faces the ground.

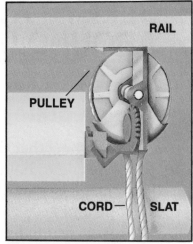

Behind every venetian blind is the magic of a pulley.

PULLEYS ARE HANDY, BUT IT'S MORE FUN TO PEEK THROUGH THE SLATS.

How do venetian blinds go up and down?

They go up and down with a cord and pulleys. To make the blinds go up or down, you pull the cord down or let it go up. This cord is different from the one that opens or closes blinds. It's threaded through a few pulleys in a heavy rail above the top slat. It also passes down through holes in all the slats to the bottom bar. When you pull down on the cord, the bottom bar is pulled up. Along with the bottom bar, up go the slats.

30

So you want to pedal your bike, sharpen your pencil, or take a dive into the swimming pool? Well, then, you'll need gears, cranks, and springs. You'll find these helpful machines just about everywhere!

TAKE ACTION WITH GEARS, CRANKS, AND SPRINGS

GET INTO GEAR!

What is a gear?

Gears are wheels with teeth. These teeth can be curved or straight. Gears do nothing alone—but they work well together! Their teeth mesh with the teeth of other gears of many shapes and sizes, like puzzle parts. Many gears working together can help you do incredible tasks!

How do the gears on a one-speed bicycle work?

A one-speed bike has two gears called sprockets. One sprocket is attached to the pedals. The other is attached to the rear wheel. A chain goes around the two sprockets. When you pedal, you turn the pedal sprocket. This pushes the chain, which turns the rear-wheel sprocket. That turns the wheel to make the bike go.

BIKE GEARS

Why do some bicycles have ten speeds?

If a bicycle has ten speeds, the rider can make the bike go fast without pedaling fast. Ten gears also help the rider pedal up a hill without straining too hard. When you ride a one-speed bike, some hills are too hard to ride up. You have to get off and push the bike. If you want to go fast on a one-speed bike, you have to pedal very, very fast, and you soon get tired. Three-speed bicycles are better for climbing hills or going fast because they have more gears than one-speed bicycles. More gears mean more possible speeds. Ten-speed bikes are even better.

How do the gears on a ten-speed bicycle work?

A ten-speed bike has seven sprockets. Two are attached to the pedals, and five are attached to the rear wheel. Each sprocket is a different size. The chain is always looped around one of the pedal sprockets and one of the rear-wheel sprockets. The bike has controls that let you move the chain from one sprocket to another. By doing this, you can get more speed or more forward force—but not both at the same time.

If you wanted to go fast on flat ground, you would put your chain around the largest pedal sprocket and the smallest rear-wheel sprocket. This combination would give you the most speed but the least force. You don't need much force to move on flat ground.

If you wanted to go up a hill without pedaling hard, you would need a lot of forward force. So you would put your chain around the smallest pedal sprocket and the largest rear-wheel sprocket. This combination would give you the most forward force but the least speed. You would go up the hill easily but slowly. Ten combinations of rear-wheel and pedal sprockets are possible. That is why the bicycle is called a ten-speed bike.

A TEN-SPEED!! YOU CAN'T EVEN REACH THE PEDALS

How do clocks work?

You'll find gears inside a mechanical clock. The hands are moved by a gear that turns once every hour. There is another gear behind the knob you use to set the alarm. On it is a special trigger bump. At the set time, a hole in the gear of the hour hand meets up with this bump. When the bump goes into the hole, the hour-hand gear moves closer to the alarm gear. This movement causes a hook holding a hammer to be pushed out of place. The hammer is released and it hits a bell. *Rrrrrrriiiiiiiiinnnngg!* When you shut off the alarm, the hook holds the hammer still once again.

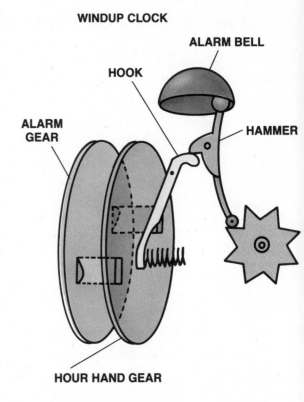

WINDUP CLOCK

ALARM BELL

HOOK

ALARM GEAR

HAMMER

HOUR HAND GEAR

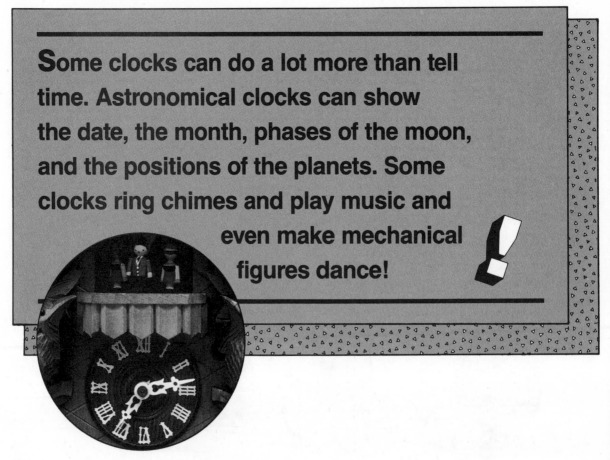

Some clocks can do a lot more than tell time. Astronomical clocks can show the date, the month, phases of the moon, and the positions of the planets. Some clocks ring chimes and play music and even make mechanical figures dance!

How do gears make an escalator work?

An escalator gets its power from a strong electric motor. The motor is connected to a gear that moves a chain. This chain is just like the chain that connects the pedals and rear wheels of a bicycle, but it's much bigger. The chain is connected to the escalator's steps. The motor turns the gear, and the gear moves the chain. The moving chain makes the steps move along tracks. Underneath, where you can't see, each step has wheels that run along tracks. These tracks are very much like the tracks that trains run on.

When a step reaches the bottom of the escalator, it goes underneath, then comes out again at the other end, at the top of the stairs. All the steps are hooked together like the links of a chain.

Escalators can move at either 90 or 120 feet per minute. Most stores use the slower speed to give customers time to look at merchandise. Escalators used in airports or subway stations usually run at the faster speed because people are in a hurry to go to exciting new places, to go to work, or to get home.

The first escalator was installed in a train station in New York City in 1900.

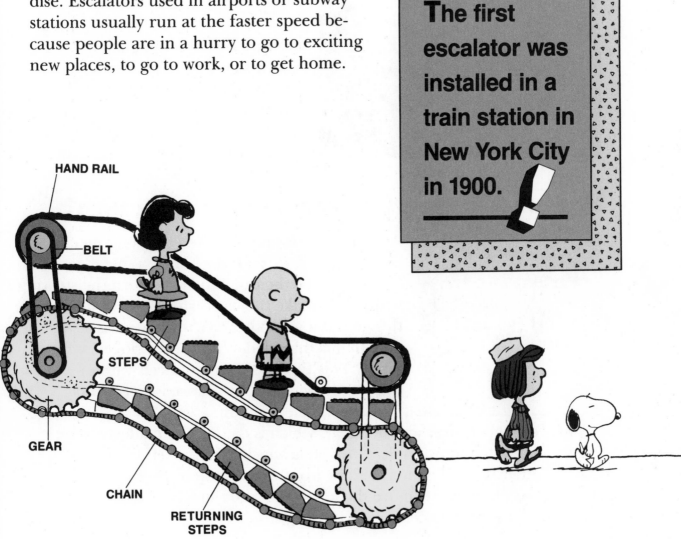

HAND RAIL

BELT

STEPS

GEAR

CHAIN

RETURNING STEPS

What makes a roller coaster go?

To get started, the roller coaster cars hook onto a chain. It pulls them to the top of the first hill. The chain can pull the cars because gears connect it to a motor on the ground. When the cars get to the top of the first hill, the hooks let go. Then gravity takes over. The cars roll down. They go faster and faster until they reach the bottom. As the cars go up the next hill, they slow down. The same force of gravity that makes the cars go faster when they are coasting down makes them slow down when they are coasting up. Each hill that the cars go up is a little lower than the hill that the cars just rolled down. This is because gravity and friction do not let the cars roll to a place as high as the hill they just came from.

How does a steering wheel make a car turn?

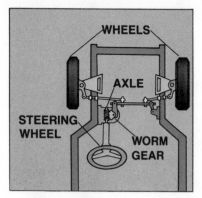

A steering wheel is connected to a long metal bar, like an axle. It extends down into a metal gearbox in the front of the car. When you turn the steering wheel, you make the bar turn a gear. In many cars this gear is a worm gear. A worm gear is a shaft or pole that is threaded—has special ridges—like a screw. This threaded part connects with one or more gears to change the speed, force, and direction of the rotation.

The worm gear turns another gear, which is connected to a lever. The lever is connected to two rods. One rod is attached to the left front wheel, and the other is attached to the right front wheel. When you turn the steering wheel, the gears move the lever. The rods attached to the lever make the car's front wheels turn left or right.

36

CRANK IT UP!

Is a crank a grouchy person?

Yes, but the word *crank* has another meaning, too. On a machine, a crank is a bar or handle that you turn in order to make a wheel or axle turn. When the wheel or axle turns, the machine works. The pedals on a bicycle are cranks. When you pedal, the wheels turn and the bike moves. The handle you turn to make a car window go up and down also is a crank.

What machine looks like an eggbeater?

A hand drill looks like an eggbeater. It has a crank and gears like an eggbeater, but instead of beaters, it has a chuck and a bit. The bit is the part of the drill that actually makes the holes. Some bits look like wood screws. The chuck holds the bit in place.

When someone wants to drill a hole in wood, metal, or plastic, here is what must be done: The person drilling holds the bit against the proper spot and turns the handle. The crank turns the gears. The gears turn the chuck and the bit, creating the hole.

Why is an eggbeater better than a fork for whipping cream?

You can whip cream faster with an eggbeater than you can with a fork because an eggbeater has a crank. When you turn the crank, it turns a large gear. This gear then pushes two smaller gears that are attached to the two beaters. As these three gears turn, their teeth hook into one another and then unhook again. Each time the big gear goes around once, the little gears go around a few times—and so do the beaters. This means the little gears are turning faster than the big gear, so the beaters are spinning faster than you are turning the crank. An eggbeater helps you by changing slow cranking into fast beating.

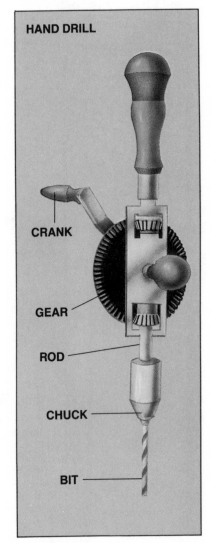

HAND DRILL

CRANK

GEAR

ROD

CHUCK

BIT

The first drill was a slender piece of wood that had pieces of sharp rock attached to it. It was invented in 400 B.C.!

How does a pencil sharpener sharpen pencils?

Inside a hand-cranked sharpener, there are two metal rollers side by side. Sharp ridges, almost like knife blades, stick out from the rollers. These ridges are for shaving little pieces of wood off a pencil. The pencil fits into a space between the two rollers. The space is wide at one end. It comes to a point at the other end. When you turn the crank, the rollers spin. They shave your pencil into the same shape as the space between the two rollers. An electric pencil sharpener has a motor instead of a hand crank.

The lead inside a pencil isn't really made of lead. It's mostly a soft, black mineral called graphite!

SPRING INTO ACTION!

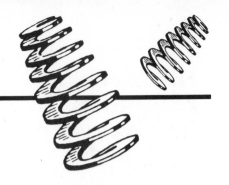

How do springs work?

Springs are used in three main ways in machines. Springs can be used to keep things in their original positions. If an object is pushed down, the spring will help pop it back into its original place. Some beds have mattresses with springs in them. The springs sink a little when you get into bed. After you get up in the morning, the springs return the mattress to its original height.

Another way springs are used is to store energy. If you push down on a spring, it stores the energy that was used to push it down. As the spring goes back to its original shape, it releases the energy, which can do work. This type of spring can be found in a clock.

Springs are also used to measure force. If you pull on a spring, the amount that the spring moves is directly related to the force that you applied. This is why springs can be used inside scales to help weigh things.

What makes springs bouncy?

Springs are bouncy because they have elasticity (ee-lass-TISS-ih-tee). This means you can stretch them or bend them or squeeze them, and they will quickly go back to their original shape when you let go. Rubber bands also have elasticity. That's why people often call them elastic bands.

How does a pogo stick help people jump high?

A pogo stick has a spring inside it. A spring, or any elastic thing, can store energy. When you jump down on a pogo stick, you use energy to squeeze the spring. The spring stores the energy for just a moment, until you start to jump up. Then the energy in the spring is let out. It gives you an extra boost and helps you to go higher.

In 1985, Guy Stewart kept jumping on a pogo stick until he had made 130,077 jumps!

HAVE YOU BEEN STORING ENERGY IN YOUR POGO STICK?

Is a diving board a machine?

Yes, a diving board is really a spring. Springs aren't always shaped like a curly piece of wire. Springs can be flat, and they can even be made of wood. Anything that bends without breaking and then snaps back to its original position is a spring. Divers like a springy diving board because it helps them to jump high. When divers jump high, they have time to do fancy tricks in the air before they plunge into the water.

How do a bow and arrow work?

The bow is a spring. When you pull back the string, you bend the bow and put energy into it. When you let go of the string, the energy is let out of the bow very suddenly. It gives the arrow a strong, fast push.

An arrow is not very heavy. You could throw it with your hand, as if it were a spear, but it wouldn't go very far. This is because your hand can't push the arrow as fast as the bow can. The faster you push the arrow, the farther it will travel. Some very strong bows can shoot an arrow half a mile!

41

What makes a music box play when you wind it up?

A music box is powered by a spring that works like a motor. This kind of spring is a flat piece of metal rolled up like a spool of ribbon. When you wind up the spring, you are rolling it tight. That also puts energy into it. When the spring is released, the energy stored in it makes it unwind and turn around in a circle. When the spring turns around, it turns a gear. This gear turns a second gear, which is attached to a roller. The roller has little spikes sticking out of it. When the roller turns, the spikes push aside thin pieces of metal called reeds. The reeds twang like strings of a guitar, and you hear music.

The highest price paid at an auction for a music box was $37,620 in 1985. It was a Swiss-made box that originally was made for a prince in 1901!

42

SORRY I'M LATE, MA'AM

OUR DIGITAL CLOCK STOPPED...

YES, MA'AM, WE HAVE ANOTHER CLOCK..

I CAN'T READ IT, THOUGH.. IT HAS HANDS

Why does a windup clock or watch tick?

A clock or watch ticks because it keeps stopping and starting again. A windup clock or watch is powered by the same kind of spring that runs a music box. The spring turns gears, which make the hands go around. If the gears kept turning without ever stopping, the energy in the spring would escape very fast. The hands would whirl around too quickly. So something called an escapement (eh-SCAPE-ment) was invented to keep the hands of the clock from spinning around too fast.

Here's how it works. Inside the clock is a tiny lever. It is shaped like a Y at one end, with two hooks at the tips. The lever flips back and forth like a seesaw going up and down. Each time the lever flips, one of the hooks catches a tooth on one of the clock's gears, stopping the hands for a fraction of a second. Then the lever flips again, letting the gears turn one tooth's worth until the other hook catches and stops everything again. Stop and go, stop and go. *Tick, tick, tick, tick.* Each tick is the sound of a hook letting go of a gear tooth.

You can see a watch stopping and starting. Just keep your eye on the jerky motion of the second hand!

How does a toaster know when to pop up?

Inside a toaster is a timer, which is just like a clock. When you push the knob down to start the toaster, you are also winding up the timer. The timer goes *ticka-ticka-tick* while it's unwinding. When the timer is all unwound, it releases a spring that makes your toast pop up. If you set your toaster for light toast, the timer will run fast. If you choose dark toast, the timer will run slowly.

Today, many toasters use a new type of timer called thermal sensors. When these sensors feel the toaster's heat, they pop up your toast.

How does a stapler work?

A stapler is like a big pair of tweezers, but something special happens when you push the two ends together. Inside a stapler is a row of staples, and pushing down on the stapler drives a bar against the front staple, forcing it through the papers. The ends of the staple are bent back when they hit a metal plate underneath. When you let go, a spring opens the stapler back up. Inside, another spring pushes against the row of staples, moving the next staple under the bar, ready to use again.

How does a bathroom scale work?

A bathroom scale uses a spring to measure weight. When you stand on the scale, you cause a bar to pull down on the spring. The spring stretches. The heavier you are, the more it stretches. As the spring stretches, a piece of metal swings down and pushes a second bar. This bar is long and flat and has gear teeth along one edge. It turns a small gear. The small gear turns an axle, which turns a wheel. The wheel has numbers printed on it. These numbers show through the window in the top of the scale. When the wheel stops turning, you see a number under the pointer. This is how much you weigh.

Do all scales have springs?

No. Doctors and nurses weigh people on scales that have no springs. This kind of scale uses a lever to measure weight. The lever works like a seesaw. When you step on the scale, the weight of your body pulls down one side of the lever. The other side of the lever has metal weights. These can slide along bars that have numbers. The doctor or nurse moves the metal weights back and forth along the bars until the lever balances. If a person weighs 82 pounds, for example, the lever will balance when the big weight is on 50 and the small weight is on 32 (50 + 32 = 82). Doctors and nurses prefer this kind of scale because it is more exact than a bathroom scale.

CHAPTER 6

Machines have changed our lives in many ways. Without them, we wouldn't have all the terrific books we read and all the wonderful clothes we wear today. Who invented them? Charlie Brown is here to help you meet some famous inventors of machines.

WHO INVENTED...?

SEWING MACHINE

MACHINES AND THE WRITTEN WORD

Johannes Gutenberg invented the printing press more than 500 years ago.

Who invented the printing press?

A German man named Johannes Gutenberg (yo-HAHN-us GOOT-un-berg) invented the printing press around 1450. Before that, Chinese and Europeans carved wooden blocks and pressed them against paper or copied the books by hand. Gutenberg's press used a separate piece of metal type for each letter. The type could be moved around to form words. Once the type was put in order, the printer put ink on it. Then he placed a piece of paper over the type and turned a giant screw. This pressed a big wooden block against the paper, and the ink left its mark.

How are modern books printed?

Computers, photography, and even laser beams are used to prepare the type for press. For printing large numbers of newspapers, magazines, and books quickly, very big automatic presses are used. Modern presses print thousands of newspapers in an hour.

Some modern printing presses are bigger than a bus and use whole truckloads of paper and ink!

47

Who invented the typewriter?

An American named Christopher Scholes invented the typewriter in 1867. He sold his invention to the Remington company, which made hundreds of early typewriters.

Remington typewriter in 1902

How does a typewriter work?

A typewriter has little pieces of metal in the shape of letters, numbers, and other symbols. The pieces, called type, are attached to levers called type bars. The buttons that you tap with your fingers are called keys. The keys are connected to the type bars by rods and levers. When you push down on a key, a bar pops up. The type hits the inky ribbon and marks the paper.

Most electric typewriters work in a similar way, but the electric motor makes everything work much more quickly and easily. Instead of levers, a central ball or wheel containing all the letters strikes the ribbon.

You can probably write about 20 words a minute. The fastest typist can type 150 to 200 words a minute!

MACHINES AND THE CLOTHES WE WEAR

Who invented the cotton gin?

In 1793, Eli Whitney invented a machine that took the seeds out of cotton. It was called a cotton gin. Before Whitney's invention, people had to take out the seeds by hand. This was very slow work. It limited the amount of cotton a farmer could grow and sell.

Whitney's cotton gin used a hand crank to turn two rollers. One roller had metal claws to pull the cotton off the seeds. The other roller had bristles to brush the cotton off the claws. Once this was done, the fluffy white fibers could be gathered up and made into thread, yarn, and cloth.

Modern cotton gins are larger and faster than Eli Whitney's, but they are based on his idea.

Eli Whitney in his workshop building the first cotton gin.

Did Eli Whitney invent anything else besides the cotton gin?

Yes. Eli Whitney invented a way of making things quickly. It is called mass production.

In the 1700s and before, people built machines one at a time. This process was slow, and no two machines came out exactly alike. Whitney changed all that. He started mass production of guns called muskets. He made batches of musket parts at once. He made all the barrels exactly alike. He made all the triggers exactly alike, and so on. In this way, a factory worker could take one of each part and put together a musket. Other workers could each specialize in making one kind of part. Whitney showed his idea to the United States government in 1798. He was hired to make 10,000 muskets for the army. Modern factories still use Whitney's idea to make almost anything you can think of.

Who invented the sewing machine?

Everyone thinks of the American Elias Howe as the inventor of the sewing machine. Howe's design in 1846 was the most successful, but it was not the first. A sewing machine was invented as long ago as 1790 by Thomas Saint of England. His machine was made for sewing leather. A tool called an awl pushed holes in the leather. A needle stitched through the holes.

ELIAS HOWE

How does a sewing machine make stitches?

When you sew by hand, you use one thread. However, when you sew with a sewing machine, you use two threads. One thread comes down from the top of the machine and goes through the eye of the needle. The other thread is in the bottom of the machine. It is wound on a small spool called a bobbin. The needle pushes the top thread down through the cloth. When the needle is down as far as it can go, a hook in the bottom of the machine catches the top thread. The hook wraps the top thread around the bottom thread, and makes a stitch. When the needle goes back up, it pulls the top thread and makes the stitch tight.

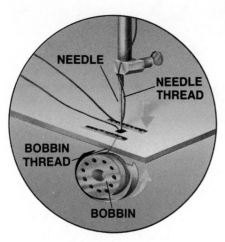

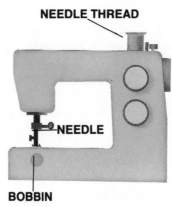

When was the zipper invented?

Whitcomb L. Judson of Chicago invented the first zipper in 1891, but the early zippers weren't very reliable. Often they jammed so that they couldn't be opened or closed. Sometimes they suddenly popped open all by themselves. It was safer to wear clothes with buttons.

Then in 1913 Gideon Sundback of Sweden invented an improved zipper that was reliable. Still, zippers weren't really around much until the late 1920s. That's when the leading fashion designers began to use them.

CHAPTER 7

Welcome to the future! Computers, video games, robots—people of long ago would never have believed the magical machines of today! The age of electronic machines has arrived.

THE FUTURE IS HERE

THE ELECTRONIC AGE: COMPUTERS AND DIGITAL DISPLAYS

What is a computer?

A computer is a machine that can remember and sometimes even learn. It has special materials in it called semiconductors (seh-mee-kon-DUCK-tours) that help it decide what to do.

Computers can be given instructions on how to do hard things, and then the computer remembers the instructions when it needs them. These instructions are called programs. People who make instructions for computers are called computer programmers. Once a computer is programmed, it can perform millions of instructions in less than a second!

LARGE COMPUTER

PERSONAL COMPUTER

How do we use computers?

Some computers tell other machines and people what to do. Spacecraft have many computers of this kind. They tell the rockets how to work and the astronauts where to steer. Other computers can play games, teach you things, help you write or draw pictures, or figure out hard math problems. You can tell a computer what you want it to do by typing on a keyboard with keys much like a typewriter. The computer responds to you by writing on a special screen called a monitor, or by printing a message on paper. A computer can be bigger than a car or small enough to fit into your pocket!

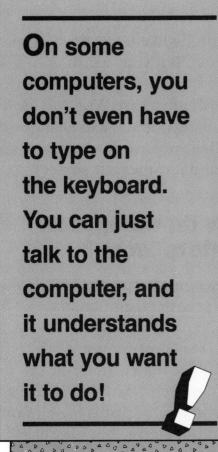

On some computers, you don't even have to type on the keyboard. You can just talk to the computer, and it understands what you want it to do!

Does a computer ever forget what you tell it?

Actually, most computers will forget what you tell them if you turn them off. So, when you turn them back on, you have to give them a new program with instructions on what to do. Some programs are kept on floppy disks, which are very thin and flat. The floppy disk is put inside a slot in the computer called a disk drive. The computer then gets the instructions from the disk and knows what to do. Some computers also have disks built right into them that can hold many programs. These are called hard disks.

What is a word processor?

Word processors are computers that work something like typewriters. You type on them the same way you do on a typewriter, but your words appear on a screen instead of on paper.

You can tell the computer to erase or add words anywhere. You can even move sentences and whole paragraphs around. This way you can change what you wrote without having to start over! When you are all done, you can tell the computer to print what you've written, and it comes out perfect.

How do computer printers work?

Some computer printers work much like typewriters, and others use lasers to print both letters and pictures. The most common printer is called a dot-matrix (daht-MAY-tricks) printer, which works like a typewriter. This prints lots of tiny dots into patterns that look like letters. Instead of a piece of metal pressing against an inky ribbon, as in a typewriter, tiny pins on a dot-matrix printer press the ribbon onto the paper. If you look closely at printing from a dot-matrix printer, you can see all the dots.

COMPUTER PRINTER

This dot-matrix letter has been enlarged so that you can see the many dots it is made of.

IF WE WATCH TV ALL THE TIME, WE WON'T HAVE TO LEARN TO READ...

IF WE USE WORD PROCESSORS AND CALCULATORS, WE WON'T HAVE TO LEARN TO WRITE OR DO MATH...

5-30

PRETTY SOON WE WON'T HAVE TO KNOW ANYTHING

THAT'S WHEN I'LL FIT IN!

© 1985 United Feature Syndicate, Inc.

The earliest electronic computer was called the Colossus. It was used in 1943 in England during World War II to break Germany's secret codes!

Is a calculator a computer?

Calculators are very simple computers. They know how to add, subtract, multiply, and divide numbers. Calculators can also help you figure out more difficult math problems.

HALF PAST A FRECKLE.

Is a digital watch a computer?

No. Digital watches use many of the same ideas as computers, but they are much simpler. Instead of the springs and gears in mechanical watches, digital watches have semiconductors in them that act as timers. Digital watches light up a display of numbers rather than use hands to show the time.

VIDEO GAMES

How does a video game work?

Video games have a computer inside them that knows all the rules and moves of the game. When you play, you tell the computer what you want to do by typing on a keyboard or by moving special knobs or levers. The computer shows you what is happening in the game by the images on its screen and by making lots of beeps and noises.

COCKPIT OF A FLIGHT SIMULATOR

FLIGHT SIMULATORS MAKE ME AIRSICK!

How do airplane pilots use video games?

Pilots use fancy video games to learn how to fly. These are called flight simulators. A flight simulator draws pictures on its screen that look like what pilots might see outside a plane's cockpit window. This allows pilots to pretend that they are flying a real plane. When a beginning pilot loses control over his "plane," the computer shows a picture of a crash, but nobody gets hurt!

ROBOTS

How do robots know what to do?

Robots are machines that can move around by themselves. Most robots are controlled by computers. Robots are helpful because they can do jobs that are tiring. They don't have to stop and rest as people do, and they can move very accurately or do a job many times in exactly the same way. Robots are also good for jobs that are too dangerous for people—like defusing bombs or working with harmful chemicals.

Robots were used in the 1700s to entertain wealthy people!

Robots come in all shapes and sizes.

Do robots look like mechanical people?

No, most robots don't look very much like people. Our bodies are so complex that we can't even come close to making a machine that does as many different things as a person. Instead, robots are made for very specific jobs and can do just a few things. The way a robot looks depends on what it has to do. Robots in factories often look like mechanical arms that are bolted to the floor. The arms can swing around to build things. Other robots have wheels so they can move on their own. These types of robots can help deliver mail in large office buildings.

57

DID YOU KNOW...?

● You've just invented a super-duper marble-polishing machine. How can you protect your new invention? Get a patent! When inventors patent their machines, they get exclusive rights from their government to make and sell the machines. This means that no one is allowed to copy their machines, and no one else is allowed to make money from their ideas. In the United States, a patent lasts for 17 years. After that time anyone can copy and sell the inventor's original idea.

● A parking meter is really a type of clock. When you put a coin in the slot, the coin drops into a system of levers. The levers figure out how big the coin is. When you turn the knob, a pointer comes into the window to show you how much time you have paid for.

By turning the knob, you also wind the clock inside the meter. If you listen closely, you may be able to hear it ticking. The clock slowly moves the pointer backward to let you know how much time you have left. When your time runs out, a flag pops up in the window of the meter.

Every week or so, a worker comes around and unlocks the bottom part of the meter. That's when he or she collects the money from the meter for the local government.

BEING A WORLD FAMOUS ATTORNEY, YOU MUST KNOW HOW TO APPLY FOR A PATENT.

PIGPEN, EVERY LITTLE MOVE YOU MAKE RAISES A CLOUD OF DUST!

I'M SORRY.. I CAN'T HELP IT

© 1985 United Feature Syndicate, Inc.   10-1

STOP BLINKING YOUR EYES!

A-choo! Because he was sick of sneezing, Melville R. Bissell came up with a great invention!

Bissell owned a china shop in Grand Rapids, Michigan. All the china that arrived at his shop came packed in dusty straw, and Bissell was allergic to straw dust. After he unpacked a shipment of china, he needed to get the dust out of his shop. Otherwise, his allergy would bother him. This was back around 1876, before vacuum cleaners were invented. So Bissell invented a sweeper with a built-in dustpan. When he used it, the dust went into the pan, not into the air. Bissell's sweepers soon became popular in many parts of the world.

● You are almost finished drawing a picture of a tree when you notice a pencil smudge. Thanks to Hyman L. Lipman, you can use the end of your pencil to erase that smudge!

Back in the 1850s, pencils and erasers had already been invented, but Lipman was the first to think of fastening them together. In 1858, Lipman took out a patent on his idea. Today, people don't have to hunt around for an eraser each time they make a mistake.

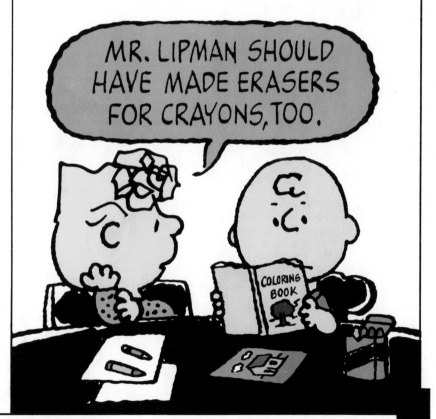
MR. LIPMAN SHOULD HAVE MADE ERASERS FOR CRAYONS, TOO.

◆ IN THE ◆
NEXT VOLUME

Have you ever wondered how the mountains were made, or what causes rainbows, or why leaves change color in the fall? You'll find the answers to these questions and lots more in volume 7, *A Guide to Planet Earth—From the Ground Up*.

My Mother Got Married
(and other disasters)

My Mother Got Married
(and other disasters)

BARBARA PARK

✦ Alfred A. Knopf, New York

Copyright © 1989 by Barbara Park
Jacket illustration copyright © 1989 by Darryl Zudeck
All rights reserved under International and Pan-
American Copyright Conventions. Published in
the United States by Alfred A. Knopf, Inc., New York,
and simultaneously in Canada by Random House
of Canada Limited, Toronto. Distributed by Random
House, Inc., New York.

Manufactured in the United States of America
10 9 8 7 6 5 4

Library of Congress Cataloging-in-Publication Data
Park, Barbara. My mother got married.
Summary: Twelve-year-old Charles experiences many
difficulties in adjusting to a new stepfather, stepsister,
and stepbrother. [1. Stepfamilies—Fiction] I. Title.
PZ7.P2197My 1989 [Fic] 88-27257
ISBN 0-394-82149-1
ISBN 0-394-92149-6 (lib. bdg.)

To my friend and editor,

ANNE SCHWARTZ,

who smooths all the rough edges,

and lets me take all the credit

—B.P.

(one)

MY PARENTS are divorced. There's no way to make it sound nice. They're divorced, and that's that.

I live with my mother, but I'm shared with my dad. It's called joint custody. It means they both want me to know that they both want me. I stay at Dad's every other weekend and on holidays and whenever else I want to. He moved into a new apartment a few months ago. It doesn't smell as bad as his first one did.

Mom and I got to remain in the house, so at least something stayed the same. The only thing that changed was our hallway. We used to have family pictures from one end to the other. But after the divorce my mother put them away in the attic. Not all at once. Little by little, like the three of us just sort of faded off the walls.

I still go up there and look at them sometimes. She doesn't know it, but I do.

A few weeks ago my mother put a picture of Ben on the bookshelf. Ben Russo. A man who's not my father. The picture's in a silver frame. Ben's smiling. So far I haven't smiled back.

My mother met Ben last summer a few weeks after the divorce was final. She was backing our car out of the driveway when she smashed into the side of his truck. We were both wearing our seat belts, so neither one of us was hurt. Ben was planting a tree in our neighbor's front yard, so he wasn't hurt either.

When he saw the dent, he didn't jump up and down or wave his fists in the air or anything. He just put down his shovel, walked over to our car, and peered in the window.

My mother was sitting there, slumped over the steering wheel. She was saying the "s-h" word. Not loudly. Just sort of whispering it over and over again to herself.

"You hurt?" he asked her.

Mom didn't look up. She just kept muttering you-know-what.

I got out of the car. "She's okay," I assured him.

(4)

"She always does this when she crashes into something."

Suddenly my mother opened her door and got out.

"Could we please not act as though I do this every day, Charles?" she snapped, her voice sounding shaky. "I've been driving for twenty-one years and this is my first accident, okay?"

I thought it over a second. "What about last year when you ran over my bike?" I reminded her. "And then there was that light pole at Dunkin' Donuts."

My mother threw her hands in the air. *"Make a list for the man, why don't you!"* she shouted at me. *"How about telling him all the things I've sucked up in the vacuum cleaner while you're at it!"*

I don't know why Ben smiled, but he did. Then he got the name of our insurance company and went back to digging his hole. The next day he brought my mother a free tree from his plant nursery.

"Trees help calm your nerves," I heard him explain as he carried it around to the back yard to plant it.

That's all it took. One free tree and they started dating. I couldn't believe it. No chocolate, no flowers—just a dumb little tree and my mother started acting as goofy as a teenager. Every morning she'd hurry out back to water it. Then she'd sigh and say, "Wasn't that nice of him?" Seriously. She said it about a billion times.

The weird thing is that Ben Russo is just about as different from my dad as you can get. He looks like one of those nature guys. You know, the kind you see in commercials walking through the woods swinging an ax and eating acorns and wild berries. He has a beard and wears boots and a belt with a big turquoise buckle. Ben Russo would look comfortable walking around in a lumberjack shirt with a squirrel on his shoulder.

My dad is more the suit-and-tie type of man. If you put a squirrel on my father's shoulder, he'd probably run around screaming, "Get it off! Get it off!"

He tried eating a wild blackberry at my grandmother's house once. As soon as it was in his mouth he spat it out and ran inside to get a drink of water.

Ben has two kids. A teenage girl and a little boy. His wife died, so I guess he sort of got stuck raising them by himself. I know it sounds sad, but that doesn't mean I automatically have to like him.

I don't exactly understand what my mother sees in him anyway. Ben hardly ever talks and when he does, it's usually real soft and quiet.

What's so exciting about hanging around a dull guy like that?

It's hard, you know? Watching your own mother start to like a man who's not your father. A guy who sells trees instead of insurance. A man who doesn't know your birthday or your middle name or where your room is. It sort of makes you queasy, if you want to know the truth.

Besides, I just always thought I'd be all the family my mom would ever need. Even with Dad gone, the two of us still had a good time together.

Like sometimes on Saturday mornings we'd go to the World of Waffles and she'd let me order the kind with strawberries and whipped cream. When we first started going, I was a little self-conscious. I kept thinking people were staring at me, wondering why there wasn't a dad with us. But after a while it didn't bother me anymore.

We went to movies together, too. We'd get popcorn or Dots or Junior Mints. Just the two of us. It was fun.

At least I thought it was.

WHENEVER something bothers me, I'm supposed to talk it over with my parents. That's the advice my psychologist, Dr. Girard, gave me. "Problems never get solved by keeping your feelings all bottled up inside you," he said.

I met Dr. Girard last year when we were going through the divorce. I'm not really embarrassed about it. Dr. Girard was a pretty cool guy to talk to. Besides, I wasn't crazy or anything. It's just that some kids don't stay as calm during a crisis as others. Like if I was ever cornered in my basement by a vampire, I wouldn't be in control enough to make a cross out of two paint sticks or shine a mirror in his eyes. I'd be too busy running around screaming.

I haven't seen Dr. Girard lately, but I still try to remember some of the stuff he told me. That's why I finally decided to talk to my mother about Ben. Sometimes if you don't talk, the pressure builds up and you can explode all over the place. Not your insides. Your emotions.

I waited until she and Ben had had four dates before I said anything. Two movies and two dinners. Until then, I'd just been trying to put up with it. It wasn't working, though. Seeing them go out together made my stomach feel funny.

Finally I just couldn't stand it anymore. On their fourth date I stayed awake until Ben brought her home. Then I went to the top of the stairs and listened for his truck to drive away.

I waited patiently while Mom paid Paul Hall for staying with me. Paul's this high school kid who lives next door. He gets paid, but he's not a baby-sitter. Baby-sitters take care of you. Paul Hall just slumps in our recliner and watches the Movie Channel.

After he left, my mother turned on the news. As quick as a flash, I was standing in the doorway clearing my throat. I already knew what I was going to say. I'd been thinking about it all night.

"I don't want you to go out with him anymore," I announced simply. "He's not Dad and it makes me queasy."

My mother jumped a foot. She scares easier than she used to.

I sat down on the couch and continued. "He doesn't fit in with us like Dad did. He's too different."

Mom raised her eyebrows. "Different?"

I nodded. "Just look at him. He's nothing like Dad. He probably goes out to the forest every morning and eats a bowl of fiber cereal."

I'm not sure how long my mother stood there staring. But finally she turned off the news and moved onto the couch next to me. Her expression had turned to puzzlement.

"You don't like Ben? Is that what you're saying?"

I shrugged. Liking him had nothing to do with it. I just didn't want him, that's all. We didn't need him.

"I don't understand this at all, Charlie," Mom continued. "Ben and I hardly know each other. We're just friends. There's no reason for you to feel so strongly about him."

I rolled my eyes. Who did she think she was kidding? Just friends? Ha! Another lie! Another big fat lie!

Parents lie all the time. It comes so easily to them, they hardly even know when they're doing it. They start you off with the one about the tooth fairy and go from there.

"Put your tooth under your pillow," they'll say when you're too young to know any better. "After you're asleep, a little fairy will buzz into your room, sneak it out from under you, and leave money."

A fairy. Yeah, right. Tell me another one.

And how about all those food fibs they tell you when they want you to eat your dinner? Like "Carrots help you see in the dark" or "Bread crusts make your hair curly."

I'm not kidding. My parents said junk like that so much, I used to think I'd end up with bushy hair and x-ray vision.

Let's face it, parents don't exactly build a lot of trust by fibbing all the time. So when my mother sat on the couch that night and told me that she and Ben Russo were just friends, it's no wonder I didn't believe her.

"The two of you were holding hands when you left tonight," I informed her cleverly. "That is not being friends. That's being something else."

She frowned. "Sometimes friends hold hands."

I shook my head. "No, they don't. Not after you get out of preschool. Martin Oates is my best friend and I've never held his hand once. Not even when crossing a busy street."

Mom paused a second and gave me a funny look. "Wait a minute. How did you see us holding hands, anyway? You weren't on the roof spying again, were you?"

Geez, why can't she ever get this straight? Just because a guy likes to sit up on the roof and be alone sometimes doesn't mean he's spying.

"I've told you a hundred times, I don't spy," I explained. "I just happened to be climbing around up there and you just happened to be down on the ground holding hands and I just happened to see you."

My mother made sort of a hissing sound. She's never been very understanding about the time I spend on the roof. Ever since I spotted her dancing with our neighbor's dog in the back yard, she's been pretty unreasonable about it.

(11)

"Remember Santa Claus, Charlie?" she asked then. "Remember the year you thought he was spying on you from the North Pole with high-powered binoculars?"

I felt my face getting red. Why did she have to bring that up again?

"It wasn't my fault," I explained for the millionth time. "It was the stupid song. The one about how he knows when you're sleeping and when you're awake and if you've been bad or good. Doesn't that sound like spying to you?"

Mom wasn't listening. "Remember how you kept turning toward the North Pole and waving? And how you spent the entire week before Christmas searching the house for hidden microphones? You thought the star on top of our tree was taking pictures."

"It blinked funny," I muttered quietly.

"Well, you didn't like it then, and I don't like it now. I'm an adult, Charles. And I deserve to have friends, just like you do. And I ought to be able to go out once in a while and get in someone's car without wondering if my son is up on the roof doing a routine stakeout."

She was making me sound ridiculous. Like a little secret agent or something. I circled my arms around my knees and hid my head.

For the next minute or two, both of us sat

there not saying a word. Then finally Mom drew a deep breath and let her cheeks fill up with air. She let it out slowly. When it was all gone, she seemed a little calmer.

"Look," she said softly. "We've both had a tough year and things still haven't completely settled down yet. But friends can help. You have yours and I have mine. And I hope that both of us keep making new ones."

I wanted to mention that none of mine would be holding my hand, but I didn't.

"Ben and I have had four dates. Four dates as friends. He's a nice man. And I like him. But most of the time he's busy with his own kids and his business. And there's simply no need for you to worry about whether he fits in here or what kind of cereal he eats."

She tousled my hair. "Come on. What d'you say?"

I looked up. What could I say? My whole argument had turned out stupid.

I shrugged my shoulders.

After that we hugged for a minute, then I went upstairs. I can't really say I felt much better. But I didn't feel any worse either. At least now my feelings were out in the open. At least now I wouldn't explode.

Not for a while, anyway.

(two)

IT WAS nine o'clock on Saturday morning. I had just gotten up. I'd been awake since eight, but when you're eleven, it's not really cool to bail out early and watch *The Smurfs*. Not even if you still want to.

When I finally made it down to the kitchen, my mother was already outside hanging sheets on the clothesline. We have a dryer but she says that sheets smell fresher if they're hung outside. It also makes them stiff as a board.

I was just about to pour some milk on my bowl of cereal when I heard a truck pull up in the driveway. I couldn't see it, but I looked out the window and saw my mother fluffing her hair, so I figured it must be Ben. A second later, she dropped the clothespins out of her mouth and ran around to the front of the house to greet him.

I wondered why he was here. To plant another tree, maybe? Or spread some fertilizer? But that wouldn't make sense. He'd already done those things the week before.

I put down the milk. If I wanted to know what Ben Russo was up to, I'd simply have to interrupt my breakfast and sneak a peek at him through the dining room window.

I was just heading into the hallway when I heard the front door slam. It was them! My mother was bringing Ben inside and I wasn't even dressed yet! I still had on my Superman pajamas! The old, faded ones that say MAN OF STEEL across the front.

I have a rule. No one except my family gets to see me in my Man of Steel pajamas. I made the rule last year after I accidentally wore them into the kitchen one Saturday morning and found this strange guy fixing the drain. His name was stitched across his shirt pocket. MAURICE. He was from France.

"Hey, Superman," he said when he saw my pj's (only with his French accent, it sounded more like "Supairman"). "Eef you've got some free time, 'ow about looking tru teese pipes and finding hair clogs for me." Then he roared for about fifteen minutes. He roared in English.

That's when I made my pajama rule. Until someone makes a dignified pair of pajamas for kids my age, no one outside the family will ever get a chance to laugh at me again.

Their voices were getting louder and louder. Oh geez, they were coming into the kitchen! I had to hide! There was no time to lose!

Quickly I shoved the milk back into the refrigerator and grabbed the box of Fruity Flakes. I learned this from watching TV. It's called removing the evidence. If I could make it to the broom closet, they would never even suspect I was up yet.

Hurry! Hurry! I screamed silently. They're almost here! Quick! My heart was pounding like crazy as I lunged for the closet door.

I made it! Just in the nick of time I was able to wedge myself in between the sponge mops and pull the door closed behind me. My foot was in the bucket, but if no one noticed my fingertips holding the door shut, I would be safe.

They entered the kitchen talking and laughing. Ben and my mother and . . . wait a second. There were other voices too. The two of them weren't alone.

"Hey! What's that?" asked a small voice. It

sounded like Beaver Cleaver. But that was impossible. Beaver Cleaver was just a TV character. And besides, he usually hung around with Larry Mondello on Saturdays.

Suddenly I felt a slight tug on the broom closet door. It caught me by surprise. I tightened my grip and tried to hold on. Outside the door I felt someone touch each of my fingers. One by one—like they were being counted.

"What are you doing over there, Thomas?" I heard Ben ask.

Whoever Thomas was, he didn't answer. Instead, he got a better grasp on the door handle and yanked with all his might. I lost my hold. And the door came swinging wide open.

A small boy stood in front of the open closet door and stared at me in wonder. His face was covered with freckles and his ears stuck out. Also, his mouth was agape. Agape means "hanging open."

His wasn't the only one, either. My mother's mouth and Ben's mouth were agape too. So was the mouth of the teenage girl standing next to them.

I'm not sure how long we stood there like that. All I know is that the boy was in serious danger of drooling, when the pressure of all that silence finally got to me.

"Boo," I muttered stupidly.

My mother's eyes widened. "Charles?" she asked, as if she had been hoping it wasn't really me.

I forced an embarrassed grin. Yup, it was me all right. It was Charles. Charles W. Hickle—Man of Steel.

Mom raised her eyebrows. "Er . . . exactly what are you doing in the closet?"

Dying, I wanted to say. Can't you see I'm dying? But instead I looked around and shrugged. "Nothin'."

Ben looked worried. "Charlie," he said calmly and slowly. It was the kind of voice that doctors use in the movies when they talk to insane people in a mental ward. "I'd, uh, like you to meet my children. This is Lydia, and that's my son, Thomas."

Cautiously Lydia raised her hand and waved a few of her fingers.

I waved my box of Fruity Flakes. It's all I could think of.

"Hey, Dad, look!" exclaimed Thomas, pointing excitedly. "He's got jammies just like mine!"

I tried to cover up, but Lydia had already started to laugh.

At last it finally dawned on my mother why I was there.

"Ohhhh," she said as the light bulb went off in her head. "I get it. You're not dressed yet, are you?"

Good, Mom. Very good.

"Listen," she said, turning to the others. "Why don't the four of us go outside and unload the plants you brought over. That'll give Charles a chance to run upstairs and get his clothes on."

Then, without waiting for an answer, she ushered Ben and his kids outside.

I have never been so humiliated in my entire life. I'm serious. Even the time I was singing in the school chorus and a big wad of underwear was hanging out of my zipper, it wasn't as bad as this.

I checked the kitchen carefully before making a mad dash for my room. When I finally got there, I shut the door, changed into jeans and a sweatshirt, and threw myself on the bed.

Why in the world had Ben brought his stupid kids over anyway? Didn't they have anything better to do on a Saturday morning? Hadn't they ever heard of TV?

And why didn't my mother warn me they were out there? Was that too much to ask? A little warning that there were strangers lurking around? Hadn't I explained the pajama situation to her after the problem with Maurice? What did

I have to do? Sleep in my clothes? Or maybe I should just lock myself in my room and never come out. That'd teach her. I could do it, too. All I needed was something to block the door, a little food, and a porta-potty.

I hadn't been brooding very long when a quiet knock on my door interrupted my thoughts.

"Dressed yet, Charlie? Can I come in?"

I couldn't believe it! She was actually at my door! What was wrong? Hadn't she humiliated me enough?

I buried my head in my pillow. "No!" I answered. "No to the first question. No to the second question. The answers are no and no."

Ignoring me, my mother took a quick peek into my room. She does this sort of thing all the time. Like a quick peek is not an invasion of privacy.

When she saw I was dressed, she opened it all the way and hurried in. Thomas was beside her. He was covering his face with his hands and peeking through the cracks. Don't ask me why, but I think he was hiding.

"Hi," she said cheerfully, pretending that nothing was wrong. "Guess who I brought with me?"

I rolled my eyes. Gee. This was going to be a tough one.

"It's Thomas!" she announced. And as she did he uncovered his face.

Golly. What d'ya know. It was Thomas.

"Thomas wanted to know if he could see your room," she explained. "So I told him, 'Why, sure you can, Thomas. Charlie would love to show you his room.'"

I frowned.

"*Wouldn't* you, Charlie," she added, more sternly this time.

Then she stood across from me and silently mouthed, "Come on. He's only five." I was still trying to figure out what his age had to do with anything when she made a break for the door.

"The rest of us will be in the back yard. Holler if you need us," she called, hurrying down the stairs.

I couldn't believe she'd done this to me! Sticking me with Thomas, of all people! The kid who exposed my pajamas to the world! What was I supposed to do with him, anyway?

He was standing in the middle of the room rocking back and forth on his heels. I looked at him, but I didn't speak. He didn't seem to mind. He just kept rocking back and forth, quietly looking the place over. Then, when he was finished, he walked calmly over to my desk, held out his finger, and started touching stuff.

He began with my pencils. Carefully he touched each of them, one by one, on their erasers. Then he moved on to my digital clock, my scissors, my high-intensity lamp, and some baseball cards that were scattered across my desktop. When he got to my globe, he held it up in the air and spun it around.

"Can I have this?" he asked nicely.

I shook my head no. He put down the globe and headed for the closet. On the way he touched three race cars on my wallpaper—a red one, a blue one, and a green one. I'm not kidding. It was spooky.

Once he disappeared into the closet, I figured that was the end of him. It's really a mess in there. My friend Martin Oates thinks there's a hand living underneath my clothes pile. He says that someday it will reach out and grab my ankles, and no one will ever see me again.

I wondered if I should mention it to Thomas. But after only a few seconds he popped out on his own. He was holding his nose.

Next he moved his touching tour to my dresser. I have a couple of stuffed animals up there, and he tried to squeak their noses. When nothing happened, he picked them up and squeezed harder. You could tell he was getting frustrated. Finally I said, "They don't squeak," and he put them back.

This whole thing took about ten minutes. When he had finished, he walked over to the window screen and hollered, *"I'm done!"* Then he sat down in my chair and patiently waited for someone to come get him.

It was Ben. I heard his boots coming up the stairs. It made me feel funny. My mother must have told him where my room was. I wondered if she had told him my middle name was Walter.

The door was wide open, but Ben knocked on the door frame. Thomas ran to him and held up his arms. He was too big to be picked up, but Ben picked him up anyway. He dangled there for a second and his dad put him down again.

Ben smiled self-consciously.

"Sorry we caught you off guard this morning."

I would have said, "That's okay," but I didn't want to lie.

After a second he turned to Thomas. "Well, can you thank Charlie for watching you?"

Thomas frowned. "He didn't watch me. I watched my own self."

Ben took Thomas's hand, but he didn't leave. I could tell by the look on his face that there was something else on his mind. Something more important than just taking Thomas back downstairs.

It made me uncomfortable. I started to squirm. It was awkward having Ben in my room without my mother along. Until then, the two of us hadn't really had a conversation. Mostly we'd just said hi, see you later, and how'd you like the movie.

"Uh . . . Charlie," he began at last. "Your mother and I were talking, and we thought that maybe next Saturday morning we could all go out for breakfast together. You know . . . the five of us."

I wiggled around restlessly on the bed. Don't say "the five of us," I thought. There are two of us and three of you, but that doesn't add up to "the five of us."

Ben cleared his throat and forced another awkward smile.

"It's just that . . . uh, we thought that it was time for all of us to get to know each other better."

Suddenly I felt sick. I bent my head and nervously started picking lint off my bedspread. I couldn't look up. I just couldn't.

He paused a second. "Um, well . . . what d'you say?"

I knew I should answer. But I couldn't. The

words he had just used kept echoing around in my head.

It's time for all of us to get to know each other. It's time. . . .

I guess it was pretty clear from my reaction that I didn't want to go to breakfast—or anyplace else for that matter.

Finally Ben mumbled, "Think it over," and left the room.

On the way out, Thomas touched all the knobs on my dresser drawers.

(three)

WE WENT to breakfast. Ben picked us up. When I got in the back seat I was very nervous. Lydia said hi. I waved. Sometimes when I'm tense, I act like a nerd.

I hadn't really paid much attention to Lydia before, but she was sitting on the very edge of the seat, so I had the chance to study her. She had the same freckles as Thomas, but her hair was too long to tell if her ears stuck out.

I wondered if they both looked like their mom. My mother told me that Mrs. Russo had died when Thomas was just a baby. I didn't know a lot of the details, but still it got to me. Having your mom die must be just about the hardest thing in the world. Harder than divorce, even.

Lydia seemed pretty normal, though. "How far away is this restaurant, anyway?" she asked as soon as we pulled out of the driveway. "I told Emily I'd be at her house at ten thirty and if we don't eat fast I'm going to be totally late."

"I'm not gonna eat fast," Thomas stated loudly. "I'm gonna eat really slow. Right, Dad? Eating slow is better for you, right?"

Lydia looked at Thomas and stuck out her tongue. I didn't want to, but it made me smile. You don't usually think of girls her age still doing stuff like that.

Thomas sat between the two of us. I tried to ignore him, but he kept staring at me like I was a freak. Halfway there, he reached out and touched me with his pointer finger.

It seemed like forever before Ben finally pulled the car into the restaurant parking lot.

"Oh, boy, World of Waffles!" squealed my mother, sounding like a little kid. "Charlie loves it here, don't you, Charlie?"

I mumbled, "It's okay," and hurried out of the car. The sooner we got this over with, the better.

The hostess spotted me coming through the door and grabbed a handful of menus.

"Good morning, sir," she said cheerfully,

knowing perfectly well that I wasn't a sir yet. "How many in your party this morning?"

"This isn't a party," I informed her bluntly.

Mom held up five fingers. "Five! We're five!" she shouted so loudly that the entire restaurant turned around to stare.

"Hey!" blared Thomas. "Guess what? I'm five, too!"

Lydia stared down at him. "We're all thrilled for you, Thomas," she said dryly.

Finally the hostess led us to a large booth in the corner. Mom slid in first. Then Lydia. I was planning to sit on my mother's other side, but Thomas beat me to it.

"Beep-beep! Beep-beep!" he honked as he plowed through Ben and me to get into the booth.

"Thomas!" said Ben. But that's all he did about it. He didn't take him out in the parking lot and punch him or anything.

The waitress brought a booster seat. As soon as Thomas climbed in, he started measuring how high his head was.

"Hey! Look how tall I am. I'm the biggest one at the table!"

Then he tapped me on the shoulder. "Hello, shorty," he said.

The kiddie menu could be folded into a pirate

hat. Thomas handed it to my mother and she fixed it for him. He put it on his head.

"Aye-aye, matey!" he sang out.

Embarrassed, Lydia slumped down in the seat. "Could someone *puhleez* do something about him?" she begged.

No one did, though, and things didn't get any better. Thomas and I both ordered waffles with whipped cream and strawberries. As soon as mine came he reached out with his finger and stole a big gob of whipped cream off the top of mine.

"Hey! Knock it off!" I blurted. "You've got your own!"

My mother turned her head and looked at me. Then she shook her head—like I shouldn't have yelled at him; like having some germy little mitt in your whipped cream was a privilege or something.

Fortunately Ben came to my rescue. "Keep your hands to yourself, Thomas," he said sternly.

After I was finished, I excused myself and waited outside on the curb. I know it wasn't polite just to leave like that, but Thomas was playing with the food on his plate and it was making me sick.

As usual, on the way home all anyone talked about was how stuffed they were. Anytime you go to a restaurant, the conversation on the way home is always the same.

"I ate too much," said Ben predictably.

"Me too," said my mother. "One more bite and I would have burst."

Just then Thomas made a loud exploding noise. "I did! I bursted! Did you hear me?"

As soon as we pulled into my driveway I opened the car door. We were still moving, but I didn't care.

"Thanks for the breakfast, Mr. Russo," I mumbled. I didn't mean it, but whenever I don't mumble thank you, I get a lecture.

I hurried up the sidewalk. The front door was locked, so I sat on the step and watched as my mother said her good-byes.

A few minutes later she came waltzing up the walk. "That was nice," she chirped. "Wasn't that nice? That was really nice."

In the next hour or two she must have said how nice it was a million times. Usually when you say a million, it means you're exaggerating. But I'm not. I swear it was a million.

Every time she said it I felt sicker and sicker. I couldn't believe this was happening. Just when my life had finally started to settle down, my stupid mother had to mess things up all over again! I know you're not supposed to call your mother stupid, but it's how I felt.

We did a lot more stuff with the Russos after that first breakfast. Picnics, a few movies and barbecues, junk like that. And even though I got to know them better—and Thomas finally stopped touching me—every time we were together the sick feeling came right back.

Just like with the divorce, I was being swept along to places that I didn't want to go. And even though my mother promised—*promised*—that she wouldn't make any decision about Ben without talking to me first, I was beginning to get nervous. Very, very nervous.

SEVEN months. That's how long it took before the announcement finally came. It was a Saturday night in February. My mother had made a big pot of spaghetti and asked Ben and Thomas and Lydia over to eat with us. After they said they'd come, she asked me if it was okay. I just shrugged. Why did she always ask *after* they were already invited?

We sat down to eat at six. Since spaghetti is my favorite meal, I was the first one finished. Thomas was last. Spaghetti takes longer to eat when you suck up each noodle like a vacuum cleaner.

Lydia shook her head. "You're such a toad,

Thomas," she told him. Then she looked at me. "He's a toad. Am I right?"

Happily I nodded.

"Use your napkin, Thomas," Lydia commanded then. "Come on, you've got sauce all over your face. Daaaad, do something. He's so gross."

Ben hardly seemed to be listening at all. He just kept fidgeting with his napkin and drinking a lot of water.

Finally, when I was just about to leave the table, he cleared his throat like he had something to say. It surprised me. Normally Ben isn't much of a talker. Ben's more a listener and a nodder.

He stood up. His face was slightly red. He seemed embarrassed and excited and nervous all at the same time. "Er . . . Janet? Could you come over here a second?"

Mom had started clearing the dishes. She put down the plates and joined him at the head of the table.

Ben smiled sheepishly. Then he reached into his shirt pocket and pulled something out.

"It's just that . . . well, I thought it would be nice if we were all here when I put this on your finger, that's all," he said softly. "All right?"

He held it up for us to see. It was a ring. A gold ring with a small sparkly diamond.

Gently Ben took my mother's left hand and slipped the ring onto her fourth finger. Her engagement one.

Mom sort of gasped. You could tell she hadn't been expecting it. I guess most people don't get engaged while they're scraping food into the sink. Then her face lit up and she looked at me and at Lydia and at Thomas. And then she hugged Ben so hard I thought I heard a little whoosh of air go out of him.

"Oh wow!" screeched Lydia, making this tiny high-pitched squeal that only girls and dolphins can make. "Oh, Janet, let me see! Let me see!"

Thomas wasn't as excited as his sister. When my mother and Ben hugged, he wrinkled up his nose and said, "Mushy." Then he looked back at his plate and tried to score a goal with his meatball.

It rolled onto the floor and landed near my foot. I picked it up, put it in the sink, and quietly left the room.

I went upstairs and called my father.

"Come get me" was all I said.

I walked outside and waited on the porch. First I sat, then I stood, then I started pacing up and down. I didn't cry, though. It surprised me, but I didn't.

By the time my mother spotted me, I was

shivering like crazy. She brought me my jacket. As she helped me with the sleeves she stopped and gave me a long, warm hug.

"I'm really sorry, honey. Ben's sorry, too," she said gently. "He didn't know about the promise."

I shrugged. It seemed shrugging was becoming my major method of communication lately.

"Dad coming?"

I nodded.

She held me a minute longer. "We'll talk when you get home."

Just then my father pulled into the driveway. He and Mom waved. They didn't end up as best friends, but at least they've been able to maintain a waving relationship.

We drove to the apartment in silence. I know it was hard for Dad not to bombard me with a million questions. Unlike Ben, my father is not a nodder and a listener. My father is an insurance salesman.

As soon as we got there he pulled out the sleeper sofa and got some pillows. It was only seven thirty, but if you're acting weird, parents like to put you to bed anyway. I gave him a funny look.

"You don't have to go to sleep. Just thought you might want to get comfortable while you're watching TV," he explained.

I plopped down and covered my head with a pillow. Then Dad brought out some popcorn and turned on the television. I stared blankly at the screen. I still don't know what was on that night.

Finally he just couldn't stand it anymore. He turned down the volume on the set.

"Is this about Ben? Did something happen over there tonight?"

I took a deep breath and nodded. There was no sense keeping it inside. It didn't feel good in there.

"They're going to get married," I managed. "They told us tonight at dinner. Ben pulled out a ring and put it on Mom's finger and—"

I stopped for a second. The lump in my throat made it hurt to talk. My eyes started filling up with tears.

"Geez, Dad. Why couldn't they just stay friends? What's so great about Ben Russo anyway?"

I looked up. My father had an odd expression on his face. Like he had just had the wind knocked out of him or something. It took me a second to realize that he was almost as upset by the news as I was. I guess it's weird finding out that your wife is marrying another man. Even if she's not your wife anymore.

(35)

He sat there a minute staring down at the floor. Like he was trying to sort out his feelings. It gave me hope. It shouldn't have, but it did.

"Maybe it's not too late, Dad," I blurted out suddenly. "Maybe you and Mom could still . . ."

But my father didn't let me get any further. He shook his head. "No, Charlie," he said firmly. "That's over and done with. You know that."

Then he took a deep breath. "I'm afraid this is one of those things you're just going to have to accept."

It made me mad, the way he said it. Like having a whole new family move into my life was just a minor inconvenience that I'd have to get used to, like a chipped tooth or a bad haircut.

I threw my hands in the air. "Sure, Dad. No problem. Just one more little adjustment in my life, right? First I start out with two parents. Then all of a sudden they get divorced and I lose my father. Then my mother backs into some guy's truck and what d'ya know, I've got a dad again. Only this one comes with a teenage sister who calls my mother Janet and a goofball little brother. And what d'ya know, all I have to do is accept it. Hey, that sounds easy enough."

Dad looked hurt. "I've never stopped being your father, Charlie. Not for one minute. Don't put that on me. It's not fair."

I turned away from him and covered my face with my hands. "Tell me about fair, Dad. It seems like nothing in my whole life is fair anymore."

He didn't answer. There was nothing more to say. Not even for an insurance salesman.

STEP—A DEFINITION

Sometimes I look up words in the dictionary. *Divorce, psychology*—words that affect my life, you know? And I wonder how they do it. The people who write the dictionaries, I mean. How do they take complicated stuff like divorce and psychology and make them sound so simple?

I looked up *step*. Not the kind of step like in a stair step or putting one foot in front of the other. I looked up the kind of step you get when your mother remarries. Like when you get a stepfather or stepbrother or stepsister. And the dictionary said: **step-** , a prefix meaning related by remarriage.

And I wondered how the dictionary could make it all sound so easy.

Why didn't they talk about what *step* really means? About how it means stepping aside so that a man who's not your father can hold your mother's hand. And how it means stepping out of the way to let a little kid scoot into the booth

(37)

next to your mother so she can fold his pirate hat. And how it means stepping over a teenage girl who has taken your favorite spot on the floor and now you have to watch TV from the uncomfortable chair in the corner.

It's not that I hated the Russos. In another situation, even Thomas might have grown on me. But I never put out the welcome mat and invited them into my life.

Let's face it. A welcome mat's just one more thing for someone to step on.

(four)

IN THE weeks before the wedding, my mother tried hard to be extra nice to me. Parents do this sort of thing when they feel guilty about something.

One week we went to the movies three times. Each time I got to have a box of Dots plus Junior Mints, plus popcorn, plus a soda. If that's not guilt, what is?

One Sunday afternoon she packed a couple of sandwiches in a backpack and we went to the park to eat them. We sat under my favorite tree. The one with branches so low, it practically begs to be climbed.

"I love you, Charlie," she said out of the clear

blue as she handed over an egg salad sandwich. She'd been saying stuff like that a lot lately.

"The important things will never change between us. You know that, don't you?"

I shrugged. "Yeah, sure. Whatever you say," I answered weakly.

Mom stopped rummaging through the backpack and sighed.

"I wish you wouldn't keep acting like this."

"Like what? I'm not acting like anything," I argued.

She took me by the shoulders. "You're acting like you don't believe me. I've told you at least a hundred times that nothing is ever going to come between you and me, and I mean it. Not Ben, not Lydia, not Thomas . . . not nothin' or nobody, no how, no way."

She laughed and she reached over and tousled my hair. "Got that?"

I couldn't help but smile a little. "Yeah . . . I got that."

We hugged. It was sort of nice.

THERE WERE only about twenty people at the wedding. My mother wore a suit. I didn't know women were allowed to wear suits to weddings, but I guess it's legal.

The ceremony only took fifteen minutes. Mom

and Ben repeated the usual junk and the minister told Ben to kiss the bride. Then my mother puckered up right there in public and everybody started clapping. Everybody but me. I only clap when I like something.

Afterward, there was a reception at a nearby restaurant. They had a band and everything. Thomas asked me to dance.

"Shh!" I said, checking to make sure no one had heard. "Boys don't dance with boys, Thomas."

Thomas frowned. "We're not boys anymore, Charrulls. We're *brothers*," he declared. Then he circled his fork over my plate like an airplane and stabbed my last bite of wedding cake. The one with all the icing.

I shoved my chair away from the table and stood up. I'd get another piece of cake. Only this time I'd sit in the men's room and eat it by myself.

Suddenly I felt someone grab my arm. I turned around. It was Aunt Harriet. The one who's married to Uncle Bunkie. The Aunt Harriet who weighs two hundred pounds.

"Come on, kiddo. Polka with your old aunt."

My eyes opened wide in fear. No, God, *please*, I thought. Please don't make me do this. Please make Aunt Harriet disappear. Zap her or something. But God must have left town right after the wedding. Because the next thing I knew, the two of us were running all over the dance floor. That's what the polka is—running all around the room while some guy named Fritz plays the accordion. We didn't stop until Aunt Harriet started getting sweaty.

After the reception, my mom and Ben drove to New England for a weekend honeymoon. Thomas begged to go with them, but my mother said that taking children on your honeymoon was something only the Brady Bunch would do.

I stayed at Dad's. I didn't see Mom and Ben again until Monday morning, when my father dropped me off at the house before school. As I headed down the hall to the kitchen I could hear the two of them eating breakfast.

When I walked in, Ben was wearing a plaid robe and slippers. He was sitting in my dad's chair.

As soon as he saw me he put down his coffee cup. "Charlie," he said, smiling warmly. I'm not sure if I smiled back. I don't think so.

My mother ran to greet me with a hug. I think I was supposed to say "Welcome home," but I couldn't take my eyes off of Ben.

"Miss me?" Mom asked, squeezing me tightly.

Meanwhile, Ben reached back to the counter

and grabbed a paper bag. "We brought you something," he added eagerly.

I took the bag and looked inside. It was a paperweight shaped like Plymouth Rock.

"It's a paperweight shaped like Plymouth Rock," he said.

I stared at it a minute, turning it over and over in my hands. "Oh," I muttered.

SCHOOL WAS a waste that day. I couldn't concentrate at all. During science Mrs. Berkie strolled over to my desk and pretended to knock on my head. "Anyone home?" she said jokingly.

Yeah, I thought. And he's wearing a plaid robe and sitting in my father's chair.

After school his pickup truck was in the driveway. It was filled with stuff. Their stuff. Mattresses, a grandfather clock, a big white desk. Furniture that would look like strangers in our house.

I guess I should have been glad they were moving into our house instead of the other way around. After all, our house was bigger, and at least I got to stay in my own room. But unfortunately there was one small problem. And it was a problem I hadn't counted on.

"You understand that you and Thomas will have to share your room for a while," my mother told me at lunch one day. "You knew that, right?"

The fork dropped straight out of my mouth. "No!" I yelled. "No! Not my room. It's not fair. My room is the only thing I'm going to have left. They're the brother and sister! Make *them* share a bedroom."

My mother's expression turned angry. "Thank you, Charles, for your wonderful generosity. Thank you for making this so easy for all of us."

"You're welcome," I said, right out loud.

"Lydia is a girl," she said then, as if this were something I didn't already know. "You and Thomas are boys."

"Lydia and Thomas are Russos," I retorted. "I am a Hickle." Clever stuff like that comes to me sometimes.

My mother took a couple of deep breaths. I think she was trying to control her voice so MaryAnn Brady, our busybody next-door neighbor, couldn't hear her yelling.

Mom put her hands on my shoulders. "Here's the deal," she informed me matter-of-factly. "When Thomas moves in, the two of you will share a room. Your room. But as soon as Ben and I are able, we will have an extra bedroom built onto the back of the house. And if you want, you can have first choice: Either the new room or your old room."

She removed her hands and started to walk away. "I'm sorry, but that's as fair as I can be right now. You'll just have to accept it."

Accept it. Gee. What d'ya know.

I'LL NEVER forget watching them move in. Ben and a friend of his from the plant nursery carried Thomas's bed up the stairs and set it down in the middle in my room.

"Where should we put it, Charlie?" Ben asked me.

Put it back where it came from, I wanted to say. Back in your old house. But instead I pretended not to hear him and went downstairs.

Later, when I came back, everything was changed. Thomas's bed was jammed in the corner by the window. A white chest with red knobs was shoved up next to it. A baby's chest. That's what it looked like. The kind that comes with a crib.

To make space, my desk had been squeezed up against my dresser, and my bed was so close to my closet that I couldn't get the door all the way open.

Sadly I walked in and sat down. I only looked around a second before burying my head in my pillow. My big, spacious room had turned cramped and teeny.

"Peekapoo!"

Thomas had crept into the room. He was lifting up the end of my pillow.

"Peekapoo! I see you!" he rhymed this time.

I groaned. "Boo," I corrected. "It's peekaboo."

Excitedly Thomas jumped on my back. "Look, Charrulls! Look at my stuff over there!"

He really liked me. I don't know why, but he did.

As quickly as he had jumped up, he jumped back down, ran over to his bed, and pointed. "See, Charrulls? I'm going to sleep here and you're going to sleep there. And it'll be just like when I spent the night at my friend Jeffrey Pete's house and then Mr. Pete had to come in four times and say 'Quiet down, boys,' and then we kept on laughing and then the next time he took Jeffrey Pete to the guest room."

This is how Thomas talks. His whole life is held together by "and thens."

As he was running around, Ben came in carrying three more cartons. When Thomas saw them, he went nuts.

"My toys! My toys! We packed them in those boxes, right, Dad? I was wonderin' where they were!"

As Ben left, my mother hurried through the doorway. She was wearing a bandanna over her hair. A bandanna means my mother's serious about cleaning. I think she wears it so she won't get mop water on her head.

She walked over to the closet and opened the door as far as it would go. Then she scanned the floor and let out a loud groan.

"I was afraid of this," she grumbled, turning to me. "This closet has *got* to be cleaned out, Charlie. Ben is going to build some more shelves. But for right now, we need to stack Thomas's toys and games on the floor in there."

I gave her a blank stare. Of all the chores in the entire universe, cleaning out my closet is the one I hate most. Besides, it didn't have to be done today, did it? Today was bad enough without adding the worst chore in the universe.

"*Now*, Charles. *Today*," she ordered, as if she had read my mind. "I want to get as much of this stuff put away as we can."

I continued to stare. What was wrong with her anyway? Couldn't she see what had happened to my big, spacious room? Wasn't that enough for her?

She folded her arms and squinted at me. "Charllllie," she said, as if lengthening my name would get me going. "The *closet*."

It made me mad. It really did.

"I can't," I said smugly. "There's a hand living in there."

It was the wrong thing to say. Mom glared at me a minute more, then stormed out of the room. A second later she was back with a box of giant plastic trash bags. She opened the first one so I could see how much it would hold. Then she disappeared into the closet and began filling it with the stuff on the floor.

I could hear it. Stuff I hadn't seen for years was being deposited in the bags for the garbage. That's where she would put it, too. My mother can be a very unreasonable person.

Just then I heard my xylophone crash to the bottom of the bag. It made me wince. I've always liked that xylophone. I realize it's a baby instrument, but I can still play "Three Blind Mice" and something else.

I got off the bed. "Okay, okay, okay!" I told her. "You win. You *always* win."

She stood up and looked at me. "You're the one who's making it into a battle." Then she handed me the bag and left.

After a few minutes of sifting through old papers and dirty socks, I found my xylophone. I couldn't find the little wooden mallet to play it with, but after searching the floor, I found a spoon. I think it was left over from a chocolate pudding I had a few months ago.

I started to play "Three Blind Mice." Just when I got to "See how they run," Thomas came back into the room. He dashed over to the closet door and started to sing.

I stopped playing right away.

Thomas finished the song without music. Then he pointed at my xylophone. "I don't have one of those," he informed me.

I knew what was coming next.

"Maybe I could have that one."

I shook my head no.

Without wasting a second, he scurried over to my desk and picked up my globe again. "How 'bout this? Can this be mine now? Can we share it?" He spun it around and around. "I really like this thing."

I put my head in my hands. I hate sharing. I know it's not the way you're supposed to feel, but I do. I don't think I'm alone, either. I think there are millions of kids all over the world who hate it as much as I do.

Sharing is not normal. If you don't believe me, just look at any National Geographic special. Name one lion who spends an entire day killing a zebra and then calls his friend over and says, "Here, Leo. I just spent ten hours chasing this zebra all over Africa. Help yourself."

Face it. The only time lions like to share is when they're already finished eating. And to me, that's not sharing. That's full.

Suddenly I stood up and hurried over to the three huge boxes in the middle of the floor. "Thomas," I said loudly to make sure I had his attention. Then I began touching each box with my finger.

"This box is yours. This box is yours. And this box is yours."

Before he could say anything, I rushed over to his bed and chest. "These are yours, too, Thomas. This is your bed and this is your little white chest. And all the stuff in the drawers is yours, too."

Thomas nodded happily.

"But that's all, okay, Thomas? Everything else in this room is mine."

I started to point. "The bed over there is mine, and that dresser is mine and all the stuff in the closet is mine, too. And the stuff on my desk and the posters on the wall. It's all my stuff, Thomas. And I'm not trading it, or sharing it, or mixing it together with your stuff. It's not even going to be both of ours. It's just going to stay mine."

Thomas was getting it now. "Oh," he muttered weakly. Then he gazed longingly over to my globe again. "I really liked that pretty blue world."

He wasn't angry. In all the time I'd known him, I'd never really seen Thomas angry. When things weren't going his way, he just seemed disappointed, and maybe kind of sad, I guess.

I softened a little.

"Okay, okay. I guess you can touch it once in a while," I conceded. "But only if you really feel you have to. And no spinning it out of control. Those are the globe rules."

Thomas smiled appreciatively and bobbed his head up and down. "I promise," he said gratefully.

He started to sit down on my bed. Then he realized his mistake and went to his own bed.

Lydia stuck her head in the door. She was carrying a small carton to her new room down the hall.

"Hi. What're you guys up to?"

Thomas frowned thoughtfully. "We're findin' out what's ours."

Lydia came in and plopped down on my bed. "Wow. You're totally squished in here, aren't you?" she observed. "Like a couple of sardines."

I know she didn't mean to be rubbing it

in—about having her own room and all—but I still wasn't in the mood to talk about it.

I left.

I hurried downstairs and passed through the living room. My mother was flitting from one corner to another trying to figure out where to put Ben's antique lamp. When she saw me, she raised her eyebrows.

"Closet cleaned?"

I nodded my head and kept on walking. I didn't stop till I was outside. I climbed up the fence and boosted myself onto the roof. Carefully I made my way toward the chimney. Once I got there, I sat down with my back against the bricks. I didn't want to spy. I just wanted to be alone.

I can't explain why, but being on the roof helps calm me down. I feel free up there or something. Like no one can get to me. And even if someone yells at me, it just floats away into space.

After about ten minutes Ben came strolling out back. My mother must have sent him to check on me. It was sort of interesting to watch how he did it. First he walked all the way to the fence and pretended to be looking at the garden. Then, trying to act casual, he slowly raised his eyes toward the roof. I stared down at him. I didn't smile or wave. I just sat and stared.

Quietly Ben walked back inside.

(five)

DON'T ASK me why, but every day Thomas seemed to like me more and more. My mother said I should have felt flattered that he followed me around so much, but I didn't. It would be like wading through a swamp and coming out with a leech on your leg. You would never really feel proud that you're the one it picked.

Everywhere I went, Thomas went. Once he even tried to follow me into the bathroom.

"No!" I told him sharply. "Not the bathroom. No."

I went in alone. When I came out, he was sitting by the door. He stood up and held his nose.

By the end of the second week I thought I would go crazy. One afternoon, just to have some privacy, I shut myself in the laundry room. I was only in there five minutes before Thomas slid open the door. He asked me to spin him around in the dryer.

Even my best friend Martin Oates and I couldn't play in private. Martin moved into the neighborhood last year from North Carolina. Since then, the two of us have stuck together like glue. My mother says it's getting hard to tell us apart. This is only funny if you know Martin is black.

Martin is about the coolest kid I've ever known. You should hear his accent. It's real slow and calm, like nobody in the world can rattle him. Also, he walks cooler than anything. Like he owns the street or something.

Thomas liked Martin almost as much as he liked me. Right from the beginning he'd follow him around the house like a shadow. Finally we gave up playing at my house and mostly just hung around the Oateses'. Martin has three sisters, but if they walk in his room, Martin throws a shoe at them, so they pretty much leave us alone.

Not Thomas, though. The few times we tried to play at my house, Thomas was a royal pain in the you-know-where. I'm serious. As soon as he'd find out Martin was coming over, he'd stand by the door to wait.

"He's coming! He's coming!" he'd scream as soon as he'd spot him. "It's that guy, Martin!"

Right after the Russos moved in, Martin came over to play Monopoly. Boy, was Thomas a pain *that* day!

"Hey! What're you guys gonna do? Can I do it with you guys? Can I? Can I, huh?" he started before Martin was even in the door.

I shook my head. "No. You can't do it with us, Thomas."

"We're playing Monopoly," Martin explained. "It's only for ages eight to adult. Look, it says so right here on the box."

"It's a law," I added just for good measure. "You could get arrested if you played."

Thomas laughed like he didn't believe me. "Hey! I know what. I can do the dice."

"Nope. Sorry. Can't," I stated clearly.

But even then, Thomas followed us into the room. He scrambled onto his bed and folded his hands on his lap. "I'll just do this, then."

I wanted to scream. Why wouldn't he get the message?

Martin turned his back so Thomas couldn't see. "Hit him with your shoe," he advised quietly.

I have to admit I felt like it. If we had been real

brothers, I probably would have tackled him and dragged him out of the room. But Thomas didn't feel like a real brother. He felt more like an uninvited guest. The kind of guest you're not supposed to clobber or your mother will kill you.

Finally Martin and I decided to try and ignore him. We figured if we didn't pay any attention to him, maybe he'd get bored and go away.

I don't mean Monopoly is boring, because it's not. Monopoly is my favorite game. For a while Martin and I played it almost every day. The best part is when the other guy is almost broke and he lands on your most expensive property and you get to jump up and scream, "Ha-ha! I'm rich! I'm rich!" The worst part is when you get into a giant brawl about trading properties and Martin throws the board out your bedroom window. So far that's only happened to us once.

After the money was handed out, Martin and I chose our playing pieces. As usual, I took the thimble and he took the shoe.

Still sitting on the bed, Thomas craned his neck to see into the box. The next thing I knew, he was on the floor sorting through the rest of the playing pieces. After touching each one, he finally grabbed the little toy iron and the top hat and scurried back to his bed.

I ignored him.

We rolled the dice to see who would go first.

"Two!" bellowed Thomas, who was really stretching his neck to the limit. "You got two, Charrulls!" He held up two fingers for our observation. "This many."

I ignored him.

Martin rolled.

"Hey! How many's that, Martin?" squealed Thomas. "That's a whole bunch, right? You got more than Charrulls. A lot more!"

I ignored him.

Martin started his shoe around the game board. Every time he touched down, Thomas counted out loud.

"One, two, three, four, five, six, seven, eight! Eight! Martin got eight!"

I ignored him.

Martin had landed on Vermont Avenue. "I'll buy it," he said.

"Buy it? Buy what? What're you going to buy, Martin? Where's your money? Are you going to use that play money, do you mean?"

This time I couldn't stop myself. I whipped around and stared at him. "I thought you were just going to sit there," I snapped.

Puzzled, Thomas looked down at himself. "I am, Charrulls. I am just sitting here. See?" Quickly he folded his hands again.

"I know, Thomas. But you're not being quiet. If you sit there you have to be quiet."

He frowned. "It doesn't say so on the box."

"Yes, it does," I said, picking up the lid. "It's right here: All children under age eight have to be quiet."

Martin grabbed the box lid and added, "If they talk, you must call the police."

Martin and I both started laughing over that one. Thomas laughed too, but I'm still not sure he knew it was a joke. Five-year-olds will believe practically anything.

For the next few minutes things got better. While Martin and I continued around the board buying real estate, Thomas just sat on his bed with his hands folded in his lap. Every once in a while I'd glance in his direction. It was a little bit pathetic, but not that much.

I was just beginning to enjoy myself when the humming started. It was quiet at first. Hardly even noticeable. But it was definitely humming and it was definitely coming from Thomas.

Ignore it, ignore it, I thought to myself. But after only a few seconds, Thomas increased the volume and added words.

"Ironing my pants . . . ironing my pants . . . ironing my pants."

I turned around. He was pretending to iron his

jeans with the little iron he had taken from the box. When he saw me looking, he put the little top hat on his head.

"How do you do, sir?" he said, making his voice real deep and tipping the hat in my direction.

Martin started to laugh. I wish he hadn't, but he did. Suddenly Thomas thought we were all having a good time. Before I knew it, he had scooted off his bed and was into the play money.

"Hey. I got an idea," he chirped happily as he plopped down. "Let's pretend that I'm the richest man in the world and that my name is Carl and that this is all my money and"—he paused to stuff some bills into his pocket—"and you guys are real poor and then you come to my house and you say, 'Carl, could we have some money?' and then I give you each two blue ones and a green one."

He stopped and handed Martin and me two fifties and a twenty.

That did it. Without even thinking, I jumped to my feet and ran downstairs. Since it was Saturday, my mother was cleaning the kitchen. She was standing next to the opened refrigerator holding something with mold on it.

"This isn't fair," I blurted. "It's not working. He's driving me crazy."

Mom made a face at the moldy thing and put it on the table. "Who?" she asked absentmindedly as she peered into the vegetable bin.

"Who? Who do you think? Thomas the Leech, that's who. Thomas the Bloodsucking Leech. Martin and I can't even play a game. He said he'd just sit there and shut up. But he won't. He counts and hums and sings and . . ."

Mom pulled out something squishy and ran it over to the sink. I still didn't have her attention.

I stormed to the phone. "I'm calling the police."

For the first time, my mother stopped what she was doing and looked at me. She was rolling her eyes, but at least she was looking.

"He likes you, Charles," she said, offering the same stupid excuse she'd used a hundred times before. "He just wants to be—"

I covered my ears. "No. I don't care about what he wants. That's all you ever say. About how much he likes me and how much he wants to be my brother. But I don't care about that, okay? I'm having him arrested."

Slowly she sank into the chair behind her and covered her face with her hands. My mother does this sort of thing a lot. Sometimes I think she's making faces at me under there.

Finally she breathed a big sigh and stood back

up. She put the moldy thing back inside the refrigerator.

"Okay," she said wearily. "I'll see what I can do. Send him down. Tell him I'll play a game of Candyland with him."

Relief spread across my face. The thrill of victory! I could hardly believe it! I'd won. At last she had listened to my side!

I was up the stairs in a flash. Breathlessly I delivered the good news.

"Thomas! My mom wants you. She wants you to bring your Candyland game downstairs and play with her."

He gave me a blank stare.

"Now! Right now!"

Without wasting another second I hurried to the closet, grabbed the game, and shoved it into his arms. "Go, Thomas! Hurry! She's waiting!"

Reluctantly Thomas got to his feet.

"Why?" he asked meekly.

I put my hand on his shoulder. "Never question adults," I said solemnly. And leading him by the hand, I ushered Thomas out of my room.

Martin and I began to laugh. We gave each other a high five, a low five, and a regular five.

The game started again. I landed on the B&O Railroad and Waterworks. I bought both of them. Martin got sent to jail. My luck was changing.

I had just landed on Boardwalk when I heard it. A creak on the stairs. Martin heard it too. We looked at each other. Then I closed my eyes as tight as they would go. No. Please, I prayed. Please don't let it be . . .

"Hi, guys."

I slumped to the floor.

Thomas was in the doorway. He was waving.

Standing behind him was my mother. A sheepish grin was pasted on her face. She motioned for me to come into the hall.

I folded my arms. This had better be good.

Casually she shrugged her shoulders. "He didn't want to play," she explained simply.

That was it? That was her excuse?

"What's that got to do with anything?" I growled. "You're the mother. *Make* him play."

Mom pulled me farther away from the door. Her expression grew more serious. "Listen, Charlie. You've got to understand this. It's not the same with Thomas as it is with you. I don't want to make him play if he doesn't want to. I don't want to be the bad guy. Not yet, anyway. Not over this."

She paused a second. "You and I have had years to build our love. We're sure of each other. Even when I'm a little hard on you, you still know I love you. But Thomas and I are just starting out. It takes time to build up that kind of love. And I just have to handle things a little differently with him right now."

She smiled weakly and tried to ruffle my hair. I backed away.

"Please try to understand," she said.

I didn't have to try to understand. It was simple. Thomas mattered more than I did. What was so hard about that?

I went back into my room. Thomas was stuffing more money in his pocket. He was already back to pretending.

". . . And pretend that I'm famous, and then you bring your little children over to see me, and then you say, 'Carl, could we have some money to take our little children to Disneyland?' "

"I'm not calling you Carl," I snapped.

Then I stooped over and dumped the Monopoly game back into the box.

I motioned for Martin. "Come on. Let's get out of here."

Thomas's face dropped.

"Where? Where're you guys going?"

No one answered.

"Wait! Who am I gonna play with?"

Martin and I were almost out the door when it hit me. I turned around.

"I know who you can play with, Thomas.

There's a hand living in the bottom of the closet," I told him. "A hand and part of a wrist under my pile of clothes. Why don't you go in the closet and let it find you?"

Thomas's face lost its color. I'm not kidding. His eyes grew as big as saucers.

I didn't stick around to find out what happened next. I just grabbed Martin and got out of there.

I know it was mean, but I couldn't help it—that's how you act when you find out your feelings don't matter to your own mother.

Anyway, it's not like I got away with it. Thanks to Thomas, when I got home that afternoon I got the biggest lecture of my life. Thomas had been so upset about the hand, he made my mother call Ben home from work to search the closet. The two of them had to go through it inch by inch with a flashlight.

That night, Thomas made Ben put Mickey Mouse night lights in every electric plug in our room. Even then, he wouldn't go to bed until I did.

"There's no hand. There's no hand," he kept muttering to himself as the two of us entered the room. "It was just a little joke. Right, Charrulls? There's no hand in the closet."

Not at night, Thomas, I thought. At night it sleeps under your bed. I didn't say it, though.

Thomas made a giant leap for his bed and quickly ducked under the covers.

"You're mad at me, aren't you, Charrulls?" he whispered after a few seconds. "You're not talking to me."

I didn't answer. I just stood at the window looking out at the roof.

"Sorry," he said.

I'm not even sure he knew what he was apologizing for.

But I wasn't about to feel sorry for him. Why should I? It wasn't just my day he had ruined. It was my entire life.

"You're a tattletale, Thomas," I told him finally. "I don't want a tattletale for a brother."

I opened the window and crawled out. "And don't follow me out here. This is the only place I have left that's mine."

Quickly I crawled to my favorite spot by the chimney. The night air was chilly, but it felt good to be out of the house. I breathed in deeply and leaned back far enough to see the stars.

Time, I thought. Time was the magic word, right? At least according to most adults, time is all you ever need to make things better. "Give it some time," they'll say, "and everything will fall into place."

Only this time nothing was falling into place. It

had been almost a month and things were just getting worse.

I was getting worse, too. I knew I was. I was meaner and angrier than I'd been in a long time.

Suddenly a small gust of wind came from nowhere and made me shiver. I pulled my knees up close to my body and buried my head in my arms.

Huddling close to the chimney, I tried to remember the last time I had felt peaceful inside, and happy. I'm eleven, and I couldn't remember.

(six)

ON THE way to school the next morning I was still upset.

"I can't believe that little nerd told on me like that," I growled as Martin and I stood on the corner waiting to cross the street. "Can you? Can you believe he squealed? What a jerk!"

But instead of answering, Martin just folded his arms and looked at me. It was the kind of look an adult gives you when you're being a brat.

"Stop doing that," I said, annoyed. "I hate it when you do that. You look like my father."

Martin didn't change his expression. "I just feel sort of sorry for the kid, that's all. You probably scared the little dude out of his skin. I bet he didn't even mean to get you in trouble. He just didn't want some hand crawling out of the closet without its body."

"Oh, great. That's great, Martin," I snapped. "Thanks for all the support."

"Don't get mad about it. I'm not saying I want him hanging around us all the time or anything. All I'm saying is you can't really blame a little kid for being scared like that. After my sister Olivia saw Frankenstein for the first time, all you had to do was sneak up behind her and she'd wet her pants."

"Yeah, I know, Martin. You've told me that before. You still make fun of her about it, too. That's how understanding you are."

Martin just shrugged in that cool way of his. "Olivia's different. She isn't human. Olivia is a creature that my mother and father created to destroy me."

We stopped talking about it after that. That's the good thing about Martin. He tells me I'm wrong and then he quits. He doesn't keep lecturing the rest of the day like my mother usually does. In this case it didn't really matter, though. The junk Martin had said stayed in my head anyway.

I thought about how Thomas was only five and

how I had been treating him and how I was new to him, too. And about how I'd known all along I wasn't being very fair to him. After all, it wasn't his fault that my mother and Ben got married. Even if I'd really hated the kid, which I didn't, I had to admit that much. Maybe not to Martin, but to myself at least.

I DECIDED to try. I'm not kidding. For the next few days I was so patient and understanding with Thomas that I almost got an ulcer from the stress. Like at breakfast, when I saw him digging his dirty little paws into the bottom of the cereal box to get the toy surprise, I hardly even groaned. And later in the week, when he got frustrated over making his bed, I helped him smooth out the lumps. All I did was take his teddy out from under the covers, but he still hugged me for it.

The thing that really got me in trouble, though, was letting him sit in the chair with me while we watched *Wild Kingdom*. It made him think we were buddies.

"Thanks, Charrulls!" he exclaimed when he got down. "Thanks for letting me sit with you. That was fun, wasn't it?"

"Yeah, sure," I mumbled as I headed to my room.

"Hey! I got an idea!" he squealed, tagging along

behind. "Want to play something? Want to play Let's Pretend?"

Let's Pretend was Thomas's favorite game. It wasn't really a game, though. Thomas would just make up a bunch of dumb stuff to act out and you'd do it. I'd seen Lydia play it with him once or twice when she was baby-sitting.

"Please, Charrulls? Please?" he begged.

I filled my cheeks with air and let it seep out. "Okay, Thomas," I agreed reluctantly. "I'll play. But only for a little while."

It almost killed me to say it, but I did.

His eyes lit up like it was Christmas or something. "You mean it, Charrulls?"

"Don't push it, okay?" I said. "Let's just do this and get it over with."

He thought for a second. "I know! I've got a great one!" he exclaimed. "Let's pretend that I'm a magic guy and my name is Carl and then you come to my house and then I turn you into a horse."

I gritted my teeth and sat down on my bed. "Okay, fine. I'm a horse. Now what?"

"No, Charrulls! That's not how you play! You've got to *do* it! You've got to come to my house!"

Already I felt my eyes start to roll back in my head. "Where's your house?"

Thomas hid behind the trash can.

"You have to knock," he explained.

I knocked.

"Hello, boy," he said in a deep voice. "My name is Carl. What's yours?"

Before I could answer, he leaned into my ear. "Say your name is Wendell."

I frowned. "Could we just get on with this, please?"

Thomas nodded. "Okay, okay. Pretend I get mad at you for knocking on my door and then I decide to change you into a horse."

I looked at him strangely. "Heck of an idea, Carl."

Thomas frowned and shook his head. "No, Charrulls. You have to beg me not to do it. You have to say, 'Please, Carl. Please don't change me into a horse!' "

He looked at me and waited.

I took another deep breath and looked around to make sure no one was listening.

"Please, Carl. Please don't change me into a horse," I said finally.

Thomas made his voice real deep. "Yes, Wendell. I must."

Then he made a loud zapping noise.

"Okay, now pretend you're a horse and your name is Jellybean."

I covered my face with my hands. This was turning out to be even more humiliating than I had imagined. "I don't want that name," I told him.

"Yes," he said matter-of-factly. "Your name is Jellybean and you're a nice horse and you get down on your knees and ride me around the room."

He stood there patiently waiting again.

I know it's hard to believe, but I did it. I'm serious. I actually got down on my hands and knees and let Thomas get on my back. We circled the room two times.

"Whoa, Jellybean. Whoa, boy," he said at last, pulling back on my hair.

"Okay," he said as he got off. "Now pretend you get mad and you try to trample me and then I poke you with a stick."

I probably don't need to mention that this was something I really didn't want to do.

Once again, Thomas waited.

I was still thinking it over when he poked me under the arm with his finger.

"Come on. Do it."

A second later he poked me again. This time I knocked his hand away.

"Hey, Jellybean! Quit that!" he ordered.

It was degrading. It really was.

"I don't think I want to play this anymore, Thomas," I said. "Thanks a lot, though. It's been fun."

Thomas started to panic. "Yes, Charrulls! Yes! You have to!"

I just knelt there, looking at him. "Sorry, Carl. I just can't," I said quietly. Then I stood up and left the room.

Lydia was coming in the front door. Teenagers are always coming in from somewhere, but they never tell you where.

Upstairs, Thomas had started screaming, "Hey you! Come back here! Come back!"

As Lydia and I passed on the steps she stopped to listen. "What's wrong with him?" she wanted to know.

"Nothing," I muttered, continuing on my way.

She turned and followed me down to the living room. "Well, if nothing's wrong, then why is he yelling?"

I picked up the remote control and flipped on the TV. "We were playing a game and I quit, that's all," I said, trying to be real casual about it.

Lydia started to grin. "Was it Let's Pretend?" she asked.

Naturally I refused to admit it.

"Don't tell me. He was making you be a horse. Am I right?" she questioned.

Geez! Had she been spying the whole time or what?

"Jellybean?" she persisted.

"Great!" I said finally, throwing my hands in the air. "That's just great. You were listening."

Lydia laughed out loud. "How could I have been listening? I wasn't even here!"

"I don't know. But Martin Oates says that girls are the snoopiest, sneakiest busybodies in the world."

Lydia just kept grinning. "Get serious, Charles. I've been that stupid horse a million times myself. Every time I play with Thomas, he makes me be Jellybean."

Hearing this made me feel a little better. I pointed to my head. "Yeah, well, guess what? I think the kid's got a screw loose somewhere."

Suddenly Lydia's whole mood seemed to change. "He does not. He's just a little boy, that's all."

I shrugged. "Whatever."

I couldn't tell if she was really mad or what. Sometimes Lydia was a real puzzle. Half the time she acted like Thomas was a pest, and the other half, she was real protective of him, like a mother would be. Once she held a Kleenex while he blew his nose. You've got to practically worship somebody to do that.

For a while we just sat there quietly staring at the TV. But I knew that neither one of us was paying any attention to it. Lydia still had something else to say. I could feel it building up in the silence.

"Thomas hasn't had it that easy, you know," she blurted out all at once. "You shouldn't be so hard on him. His life has been hard enough."

I squirmed in my chair. It was embarrassing, being yelled at like that.

"He never even knew our mother," she went on. "Just think what that must be like for a minute."

She paused, and her voice softened. "She was really cute, my mom was. She didn't look like a grown-up woman, exactly. More like a kid. That's where Thomas and I got our freckles. Daddy says she had one of those faces that never get old."

She stopped again, as if she were remembering. "Thomas was only six weeks old when she, well, when she got sick. He looks at her pictures sometimes. He knows that it's Mom. We've told him enough. But still, you can tell by his eyes that he's looking at a stranger."

I glanced over at her face. Her eyes were filling up with tears.

She wiped them and stared out into space.

"It's really hard, you know?" she added almost

in a whisper. "When I fill out forms at school, I write 'deceased' where Mom is supposed to go."

Tears started to run down her cheeks. This time she stood up and hurried out of the room.

"Sorry," she said. "Sorry."

"No . . . it's okay," I called after her. "Really."

I wished I could have told her that I understood. I didn't, though. How could I? How could anyone understand something as sad as that?

(seven)

THE NEXT day things seemed to be back to normal. Lydia's alarm went off at six A.M. Then, just like every other school morning, I heard her come padding down the hall in her fuzzy bunny slippers. The ones with the ears. Then the bathroom door closed and the sound of the lock echoed in the hallway.

That was that. Lydia wouldn't come out again until her ride to school started honking the horn. Even if Thomas and I had to go really bad, she wouldn't unlock the stupid door. The first week she moved in I made a wet spot on my Superman,

Man of Steel pajamas. I'll never really forgive Lydia for that.

The trouble was, even when I did get into the bathroom, it wasn't the same as it used to be. Makeup and hair junk and perfume were crammed everywhere. Sometimes there was so much crap I couldn't even find my toothbrush. Once when I picked it up, it had already been used. I still get queasy when I think about it.

Besides the bathroom mess, rubber bands with little hair balls in them could be found all over the house. Like suddenly, she would be walking through the house and get this uncontrollable urge to rip out her ponytail, hair and all. It was disgusting and scary at the same time.

There was one more thing, too. Lydia smelled. I'm not kidding. She would walk by, and suddenly this giant perfume cloud would fill the air and make you cough. It hung in the air for about twenty minutes. To breathe, you had to put a hanky over your nose.

I'm not exaggerating. One night at dinner Ben took a whiff of her and pretended to clear out his sinuses. Lydia got tears in her eyes and left the table.

She ran upstairs to take a bubble bath. She took at least two baths or showers a day. That's twice as many as I took the entire time I was at camp.

"Great!" she shrieked from the top of the stairs. "Thomas used all my bubble bath again! There was almost half a bottle left last night and now it's gone!"

Ben glanced at Thomas and frowned.

Thomas shrugged and shoved in another forkful of mashed potatoes.

"Did not," he mumbled.

Lydia stormed back down to the kitchen and held the empty bottle upside down.

"Look at this! It's totally gone! He must have had bubbles up to the ceiling!"

Thomas kept right on eating.

"Did not," he repeated quietly. A kernel of corn fell out of his mouth onto the place mat.

"Yes, you did! You did too!"

This time Thomas looked up and smiled. "Not, not, not," he said.

"Too! too! too! too! too! too! too!" shrieked Lydia.

I excused myself from the table. Fights at dinner cause indigestion. And besides, I had enough problems of my own without getting involved in this one.

But just in case anyone wants my opinion, if Lydia had wanted to keep her precious bubble bath to herself, she shouldn't have put it right out on the tub in plain sight. It's not like it had her name on it or anything. Who knew?

And anyway, if the stupid bubbles had lasted longer, I wouldn't have needed so much.

UNFORTUNATELY, Lydia hogged more than just the bathroom. She was also a telephone hog. I'm not sure which was worse. When you think about it, the telephone and the toilet are a lot alike. You might not use them that often, but when you need them, you *need* them.

One night, because of Lydia's blabbing, I had to walk home from Martin's house in the pouring rain. I tried for an hour and a half to call my mother to come get me. That's ninety straight minutes! And all I could get was a busy signal!

Getting a busy signal for an hour and half makes a person crazy. I'm not kidding. I read about a guy who got so mad at a busy signal that he shot his telephone right in the receiver. He said it was self-defense. I can understand that now.

Anyway, it finally got to be dinnertime and I was forced to leave. Mrs. Oates invited me to stay, but she was having vegetable casserole. I had it once. It made me spit up.

By the time I walked the two blocks to my house that night, I was soaked and shivering.

Also, my underwear was blue from my wet jeans.

Lydia was off the phone and back in the bathroom. Ben made her get out so I could take a hot bath. When she walked past, I gave her a dirty look.

"Thanks for staying on the phone all night," I growled.

Lydia looked at me and gasped.

"Oh wow! That reminds me. I haven't called Amanda back yet!"

I wore the underwear in the tub, but the blue never came out.

THE NEXT week I came down with the flu. I got it from the rain. My mother said you can't catch the flu from the rain but I did.

Ben and Lydia caught it first. I don't know where they got theirs, but they both got sick on Sunday. I didn't get sick until Wednesday. By then, all of my mother's sympathy had already been used up.

"You don't have a temperature," she informed me Wednesday morning when I said I didn't feel good.

"I don't care. I'm still sick," I told her.

She checked the thermometer again. "Why don't you go to school and give it a chance? See how you feel at lunchtime," she suggested.

I shook my head. "I can't. I'll be dead by lunchtime."

This time she frowned. "I want you to give it a try, Charlie. I've got to go into the office today and Ben's got his hands full with Lydia. Two sickies is just about all this family can handle."

"Oh, excuse me," I snapped. "Next time I'll wait my turn so I won't inconvenience anyone."

"Don't be so dramatic," Mom continued. "You know how you are. Sometimes after you get moving around a little bit, you start feeling better. If you don't, you can call me at work. You know the number of the real estate office, right? If you call, I'll come get you. I promise."

There was no sense arguing. Her mind was made up. I was going to school and that was that.

It turned out just like I knew it would. By eleven o'clock my head was down on my desk. By eleven fifteen, I was scouting the room for emergency places to puke.

Suddenly I shot my hand into the air. My stomach told me to.

"I need to go to the nurse's office!" I blurted out from the back of the room.

My teacher looked up from her desk.

"Now!" I added urgently.

Mrs. Berkie got the message. She sprang up

from her seat, dashed down my aisle, and slapped a hall pass into my hand.

"Run like the wind," she told me.

Out in the hall I could smell the food from the cafeteria. Beef and bean burritos. I put my hand over my mouth and started booking down the hall.

By the time I hit Nurse Cook's office I was almost out of breath. I didn't even wait for her to ask what was wrong. I just flopped down on her cot and rolled up into a little ball.

She stared at me a moment, but I can't really say she looked surprised. I have a feeling that on beef and bean burrito day, scenes like this are pretty common.

She covered me with a blanket and put her hand on my forehead. "Not feeling too good, huh?" she asked.

"Your name?"

I moaned and answered at the same time.

"Stay here. I need to go get your emergency card," she said. "Be back in a minute."

A minute? Oh no! I couldn't last a minute! Deep breaths, I ordered. Lots of deep breaths and the sick feeling will go away. In and out . . . in and out . . . in and . . . up. It came up on breath number three. I barely had time to grab the trash can.

The nurse came back before I was finished. She stopped in the doorway and made a face. Personally, I think that this was very unprofessional.

"Are you okay?" she asked at last.

Oh, yes. I'm fine, I thought. I love barfing into school trash cans. It's a hobby of mine.

But instead of saying anything, I just nodded.

Nurse Cook gave me a wet paper towel and pointed me toward the sink. Then she held her breath and carried the can out of the room.

A few minutes later she phoned my mother at work.

"Sorry, hon, but your mother isn't in the office right now," she reported. "They say she's out looking at property."

She tried my father next. He wasn't in his office either.

I sighed deeply. "Try my house," I suggested weakly.

She stared curiously at my emergency card again. "But if both your parents work, who would be at home?"

I took a deep breath. I had no choice. I was finally going to be forced to say the word.

"My stepfather," I replied, feeling sicker than ever.

Nurse Cook dialed the number. "Busy," she reported. "I'll try again in a few minutes."

She did, too. She tried calling my house for more than an hour. But every single time her message was the same. "Sorry, hon," she'd say. "Your phone is still—"

"I know. You don't have to tell me. Busy," I would mutter weakly.

By one o'clock my head was splitting and I had the chills. I tried to stay warm, but every kid who wandered into the office lifted up the blanket to see who I was.

At one thirty, Nurse Cook drove me home. I think she was afraid I was going to die on her cot. When you're a nurse, you have to worry about stuff like that. A death doesn't look that good on your record.

I was never so glad to see my house in my life. All I wanted was to go upstairs, crawl under my covers, and shiver in private. I dropped my books on the first step and started up to my room.

"That you, Charles?" called Ben, sounding raspy. "School out early?"

Slowly I turned around. Then, holding my head so it wouldn't explode, I walked gently into the living room.

Ben was stretched out on the couch watching TV. He was covered by a giant quilt. Lydia was curled in a big pink blanket next to the phone. The receiver was slightly off the hook.

I stood there and stared in disbelief. She had probably been talking to one of her sick friends and hadn't hung it up all the way. I couldn't believe it. All this time and no one had even noticed. Hadn't they heard the loud beeping the phone makes when it's off the hook? How could anyone sleep through a racket like that?

I should have started yelling. After what I'd been through, I should have yelled my brains out. But I just couldn't. If I yelled, my head would have split open.

I started out of the room. Ben looked sort of green. "Wait. So, how was your day?"

This time I couldn't resist. "Great. It was just great, Ben. I ralphed in the nurse's trash can."

Then I turned toward Lydia. "Oh yeah," I added. "Nurse Cook tried calling, but . . ."

I pointed at the phone.

Right away, they both saw the problem. Lydia got this sheepish look on her face. "Whoops. Sorry," she said, replacing the receiver. "I didn't hear it beep or anything. I must have been in the bathroom."

Ben frowned at his daughter. "Lydia," he said sternly. But that was it. I'm serious. That's all the punishment she got.

After that I went right to my room and got into bed. Then I burrowed my head in my pillow and tried not to die until my mother came home.

She walked through the front door at four o'clock. Ben must have told her what happened. At four thirty she brought hot tea and chicken noodle soup up to my room on a tray.

"I'm working on the Jell-O," she told me. Then she sat down on the edge of my bed—carefully, so she wouldn't spill the soup—and gently rubbed the side of my cheek with her hand.

She put her forehead next to mine and smiled sympathetically. That's one good thing about my mother. Even when I'm contagious, she's never afraid to get close to me.

"Sorry about what happened today," she said softly. "You okay?"

"No. You promised you'd be there and you weren't."

"I know, Charlie. I'm sorry. I was called out of the office unexpectedly and—"

"I knew this would happen. I told you I was sick but you wouldn't believe me. You didn't even care."

My mother looked as guilty as anything. "I cared," she said, rubbing my cheek again. "I know you had a bad day, honey, but—"

A bad day? Was that the understatement of the year or what?

I rolled my eyes. "Losing your favorite pencil is a bad day, Mother," I interrupted. "Puking in a trash can is just a little more serious."

My mother knows when she's licked. She didn't bother making any more excuses. Instead, she just sat there quietly while I ate my soup.

Ben and Lydia called her. She shouted, "Be there in a minute!" but she didn't go right away.

For a little while, it was just her and me.

(eight)

I SPENT the weekend at my dad's. I still wasn't feeling great, but anything was better than being home with Thomas. At least my father didn't keep coming into my room saying "Pretend that I'm a doctor and my name is Carl and I get to give you a shot."

My dad tried to understand what I was going through. Even when I was sick and grouchy he was pretty patient with me.

"I hate it there. I hate it," I complained again and again. "Living with the Russos is like living in a loony bin. Thomas is actually a man named Carl and Lydia has a phone growing out of her ear."

Dad surprised me. Ordinarily he would have put his hand on my shoulder and said something like, "Oh, come on, son, it's not that bad." Or, "Just give it a few weeks, it'll get better." But this time he really caught me off guard.

He took a deep breath and let it out slowly. "If I could have you here with me, I would. I hope you know that."

For a split second my whole world lit up. Just the thought of it was enough to change my mood.

"Dad! That's it! Of course! That's the answer to my problems! I'll come here and live with you! Just you and me. It'll be great! Why didn't we think of this before?"

Dad looked puzzled. "We did, Charlie. We talked about it with your mom before this all happened. You said you didn't want to leave your old neighborhood or change schools or stay with a baby-sitter when I'm out of town."

He paused a second, as if he was trying to recall something else. "Oh yeah, and you weren't too crazy about the idea of sleeping in the living room forever either. Don't you remember that? It wasn't even that long ago."

Suddenly my world crashed back in on top of me again.

"Yeah . . . I remember," I said, glumly staring at

his pull-out couch. "I just forgot for a second, but I remember now."

It was pretty obvious that I was disappointed. Dad reached over and gave me a quick hug.

"Never any easy answers, are there, son?" he asked sympathetically.

I shook my head no. Not anymore, I thought sadly. Not since last year when you left.

I DIDN'T go home until four o'clock on Sunday. I would have stayed at Dad's for dinner, but he was having shrimp egg rolls, beets, and stewed tomatoes. Men eat like that when they're alone.

When I walked into the living room that afternoon, Mom and Ben were sitting on the couch. Thomas and Lydia were stretched out on the floor in front of them. Seeing them like that sort of took me by surprise. They just looked so much like a normal family without me there.

I stood in the doorway with my suitcase. The extra son with the extra father.

"Oh, good, Charlie!" my mother exclaimed when she saw me. She hurried over and gave me a hug.

In her hand was a magazine. "There's a great article in here. I found it in the dentist's office yesterday and I've been waiting for you to get home so I could read it to everyone."

I didn't bother to argue. My mother takes her magazine articles very seriously.

She clicked off the TV and looked around. "Is everybody listening? It's called 'Bonding with Your Stepchildren.'"

Thomas bolted up. He'd been watching some wildlife show and was pretty annoyed that Mom had just clicked it off.

"Hey! What happened to the snakes?" he hollered.

My mother smiled.

"In a minute, Thomas. Right now this is more important. The doctor who wrote this is a psychiatrist with five stepchildren. He's had a lot of experience with families like ours—you know, stepfamilies—and he's made some suggestions that I thought might be good to try."

Ben shifted uneasily in his seat.

"I'd rather watch the snakes," whined Thomas.

"Shh," shushed my mother, and she began to read.

"'It's a good idea for each parent to spend time alone with his or her new stepchild. This should be quality time set aside for just the two of them. By joining in a favorite activity together, they can get to know each other away from the pressures of the family. They can learn to confide in each other. Learn to trust. And it's through this trust that the bonding process can begin. . . .' "

When she had finished, Mom looked up from the magazine and beamed proudly. I'm not kidding. It was like she wrote it herself or something.

"Well?" she asked. "What do you think?"

Ben was still fidgeting. Slowly he shook his head. "I don't know, Janet. I think we're doing fine the way we are. Isn't it better to learn to blend together as a family than to split everybody up?" he asked.

Thank you, Ben, I thought secretly. Thank you for wanting to spend quality time alone with me.

Meanwhile, my mother looked up at the ceiling and grimaced.

"Spending time alone with each child is not splitting everybody up, Ben. If Thomas and I spend some time alone and we get to know each other better, how can that possibly split things up?"

Mom looked at Lydia and me. "What do you two think? Lydia? Charlie?"

Lydia shrugged. She was right in the middle of pulling one of her rubber bands out of her head.

I just stared blankly into space. Maybe sleeping on the couch at Dad's wouldn't be so bad after all. At least my father didn't need to be forced to love me.

Suddenly Thomas got up off the floor and stormed over to where my mother was sitting. Then he leaned right into her face.

"I said I want to watch the snakes, dammit!"

Hearing him swear took all of us by surprise. A big hush settled over the room and my mother's mouth dropped open. So did mine.

I tried to keep from laughing, but it wasn't easy. Especially when Ben grabbed Thomas by the arm and marched him up the stairs. Thomas knew he was in big trouble. The whole way to his room he kept saying, "I don't *have* to watch the snakes, Dad. Let's be friends. Do you want to be friends, Dad?"

When Ben finally came back downstairs, he walked over to my mother and put his arms around her. He did it right in front of Lydia and me.

"Looks like maybe we'd better give this guy's idea a try," he said, picking up the magazine.

Mom rested her head on his shoulder and whispered, "Thanks."

I left the room. It bothered me to see the two of them hug. I wouldn't have minded if Ben had given her a hearty slap on the back once in a while, but soft whispering and hugging—well, it just got to me, that's all.

THEY SET it up for Saturday. Ben and I would go fishing and Mom would take Lydia shopping and out to lunch. Thomas would go to his friend Jeffrey Pete's house. His turn would come next.

The more I thought about it, the less I wanted to go. What kind of personal junk was I supposed to learn about Ben, anyway? That he liked to stomp around in nature in a flannel shirt and eat Hungry Jack pancakes? That he went outside every night after dinner and watched the sun set? Okay, fine. So what?

And what about me? Was I actually supposed to confess my true feelings about his family? Should I tell him that I thought his son was a mental case, or that sometimes Lydia was unbelievably selfish? Would that "bond" Ben and me together?

Or how about this one? Would it help if I told Ben that sometimes when no one was around I went up to the attic and pulled out the box of pictures my mother had put away? The ones of her and Dad and me. And that I stared at them and tried to remember.

And that sometimes my eyes clouded up. Not

often, but it still happened. Should I tell him that, too?

BEN HONKED his horn. Reluctantly I walked downstairs and closed the front door behind me.

I got into the truck. Ben leaned over and gave me a pat on the knee.

I forced a smile, but it wasn't easy. The thing is, I don't even like fishing. It was Ben's idea. I know this doesn't make me seem like much of an outdoorsman, but it's true. The first time I ever went fishing I hooked my father in the neck and he took my pole away. The second time I caught a pair of boxer shorts and a plastic bag.

Ben pulled out of the driveway and turned on the radio. "Thought we'd go to Lake Murky," he said. "Ever been there?"

I nodded. Lake Murky. That's where I had caught my boxer shorts.

It wasn't a very long drive but the two of us didn't talk much. Ben and I never do. My mother says he's not much of a talker, but I couldn't help wondering if he just didn't like me. Once the two of us were stuck in the car while Mom ran into the grocery store. Ben cleared his throat twice. It was one of our best conversations.

When we finally got to the lake, we unloaded the fishing gear from the back of the truck. Then we walked down to the boathouse. Ben bought some sandwiches and other stuff from the cooler and then rented a small motorboat.

You could tell he'd done a lot of fishing up there. Once we were in the boat, he knew right where to go. He drove to this little cove about ten minutes from the dock and turned off the engine.

"Best fishing spot on the lake," he informed me as he handed me a pole. Then he reached into the bait box and pulled out a fat wiggly red earthworm. It was the slimy kind that are squished all over the sidewalk after a hard rain.

"Here you go," he said.

I felt myself start to sweat. There aren't a lot of guys who will admit this, but worms sort of turn my stomach. I think it has something to do with them not having arms, legs, or a neck.

For a second or two I didn't know what to do. I tried to hold out my hand, but it just stayed tucked under my arm in a tight little fist. Meanwhile, Ben kept stretching his arm farther and farther for me to take it.

Finally I shook my head. "Er, no thanks. I, uh, don't use worms. I usually just use . . . well, uh, I just use . . ."

Geez, why couldn't I say it?

Curiously, Ben raised his eyebrows. He was waiting.

I ducked my head down and mumbled "Bologna" as quietly as I could into my sleeve.

Ben stared at me a second. "Bologna?" he repeated loudly. I'm not kidding. The word *bologna* echoed all over the lake.

I could feel my face turning red. What was the big deal, anyway? Last year Martin Oates caught a sea bass with a Vienna sausage.

Ben looked at me funny but he didn't laugh. "Sorry. No bologna. Try this."

He tossed me a fudge brownie that he'd bought at the boathouse. I tore off a small piece and rolled it into a ball. Then I put it on the end of my hook. I felt like I was fishing for Betty Crocker.

For the next two hours the two of us just sat there with our poles in the water. Some fun. Most of the time I think Ben was practically asleep. Once in a while, when my bobber would move, he'd open his eyes and say, "Got a nibble?" But it didn't actually make me feel bonded to him or anything.

Ben was the first to get a bite. As soon as he felt the tug on the line he sat up and began reeling it in—steady and calm like you're supposed to.

But even though he wasn't jumping up and down, you could tell he was getting a kick out of it. The whole time he was pulling it in, he kept whispering "Come to Papa, come to Papa."

"Get the net, Charlie," he ordered. "Quick! Scoop him in."

I leaned over and caught the fish in the net. It was flopping around like crazy.

I cringed when I saw the hook. "Gross," I said. "Right through the lip."

Ben took the fish and tried to twist the hook out of its mouth. Suddenly I felt queasy.

He looked up and saw my expression. "Don't worry. It doesn't hurt him."

"How do you know?" I asked.

Ben just kept twisting.

I covered my eyes with my hands. "It's kind of hard not to feel a hook through your mouth, don't you think?"

Ben didn't answer.

"I even feel it when I've got a crumb on my lip."

After a minute I peeked through my fingers. "Sure looks like it hurts, doesn't it? The way it keeps flopping around like that."

I leaned closer. "Oh geez, it's bleeding."

Seeing the blood made things even worse.

"What's the difference between fishing and murder, do you think?" I wondered out loud. "Do you think just because you eat it, it's not murder?"

Ben stopped what he was doing and stared at me. He didn't say anything. He just stared.

Finally the hook came out. "My guess would be that you won't be wanting to take this home and eat it, is that correct?" he asked, sounding a little exasperated.

I made a face at the thought of it. "You mean with that lip of his and everything?"

Ben threw it back. Then for the next few minutes he just sat there looking out over the water.

I guess I shouldn't have made him throw it back. I guess we should have taken it home and eaten it. I probably wouldn't have had to eat the lips.

Hoping to make things better, I cast my brownie back into the lake. Five minutes later I caught a Huggies diaper.

Ben started the outboard motor. We left.

On the way home the silence was louder than ever.

(nine)

THE LAST straw. That's what they call it when you run out of patience. I never used to understand why they called it that, but I do now. It's like if you're a camel and you have to carry a bunch of straw to market. And everyone thinks you're real strong, so they just keep piling more and more straws on your back. And even though your load keeps getting heavier and heavier and your legs start buckling underneath you, you just put up with it, because that's what they expect you to do.

Only finally you reach your limit. You don't know it's going to happen. But one day someone reaches up and puts one more straw on your back, and you collapse right on top of him. And he deserves it too. 'Cause he wasn't paying attention to how you felt. And everyone has a limit. Me and camels and everyone.

THOMAS started calling my mother Mom. He started doing it after their day "alone" together. I don't know if they talked about it or if he just did it on his own. All I know is that he was heading up to bed that night when he suddenly stopped on the stairs and said, "See you in the morning, Mom."

I'm not kidding. He said it real casual like that. As if calling a person Mom was hardly a big deal at all.

It really got to me. *Don't call her that!* I wanted to shout. She's my mother, not yours!

I THOUGHT about it that night. Not just about Thomas calling my mother Mom. I thought about all of it. About Lydia and Ben, and how much I'd given up, and how much I'd had to accept: sharing my room with a little kid, learning to live with a sister, giving both of them my mother, watching her love a man who wasn't my dad—a man who didn't even seem to like me that much. . . .

It felt heavy, you know? Like a ton of straw,

only worse. And even though I was in bed, I thought I felt my legs start to buckle under me. I'm serious. I could really feel them caving in.

I didn't sleep very well. I tossed and turned and woke up a million times.

Glum. That was my mood when I went down to breakfast the next morning. Not a good time to discover that Lydia and Thomas had eaten the last bowl of Fruity Flakes. When I looked in the cupboard all that was left was Ben's cereal. Fiber something.

I hurried into the living room and there they were. Thomas was curled up in the chair watching *Sesame Street*. Lydia was stretched out on the couch waiting for the phone to ring. They both looked full.

"Look, Charrulls," said Thomas excitedly as he pointed to the screen. "There's Bernie!"

I rolled my eyes. "How many times do I have to tell you, Thomas?" I said. "It's not Bernie. It's Bert and Ernie. They're two separate people."

"Puppets," corrected Lydia, raising a finger in the air.

I frowned. "Oh. Like I didn't already know that."

Just then my stomach started to growl. Not loud enough for anyone to hear, but enough to make me double over.

Lydia glanced at me curiously.

"My stomach's growling," I informed her curtly. "The reason it's growling is that no one left me anything to eat for breakfast. All the cereal's gone."

Casually she shook her head. "That's not true. There's other cereal in there."

I made a face. "Oh, boy. Bark and twigs."

Lydia shrugged again and turned back to the TV.

"The Fruity Flakes were mine," I persisted. "My mother bought them for me."

This time she looked at the ceiling and sighed in annoyance. "They were for *all* of us, Charles."

"No, they weren't," I argued. I could feel the anger building inside me. "They were just mine. I get to have something around here too, you know. You two don't get everything!"

Lydia's eyes grew wide. "Everything?" she snapped, bolting up. "What do you mean we '*get everything*'? What have we cheated you out of, Charlie? We gave up our whole house and our whole neighborhood to come here. What did you give up? Nothing, that's what! So excuse me if I accidentally had the last bowl of cereal, Your Majesty!"

I was trying to think of something smart to yell back at her when Thomas stamped his foot.

"Shh! Quiet!" he shouted. "I can't hear the Bernie with the long head!"

I covered my face with my hands. Like I said, the place was a loony bin.

"Bert," I muttered for the millionth time. "His name is Bert. Bert, Bert, Bert, Bert, Bert, Bert, Bert, Bert . . ."

Beep-beep! Outside, a loud car horn interrupted my Berts. I don't mean just one or two little toots, either. I mean major honking. Like little kids do when their mom leaves them in the car while she runs into the grocery store.

Thomas stood up in the chair and peeked through the window. "*Meemee!*" he shrieked. "*Meemee Russo!*"

The next thing I knew, he and Lydia were flying out of the living room headed toward the front door. That was that. I never even had a chance to finish my argument with Lydia. I could have thought of some good stuff, too. I know I could have.

Feeling more frustrated than ever, I stood up and looked outside. The honking was coming from a giant white car parked in our driveway. I'm not sure of the make, but it was the kind of car they call a gas guzzler. I'd seen it before at the wedding.

It belonged to Ben's mother.

In the time it took me to get to the window,

Mom and Ben had dashed from the back yard to greet her. Standing there with Thomas and Lydia, Ben opened her door.

Mrs. Russo got out of the car. Her cotton-candy white hair came first, about two feet of it piled on top of her head. It was the kind of hair that you could shoot a cannonball through and never get close to her scalp.

She hugged and kissed each one of them. Thomas's hug was the longest. He dangled from her neck until Ben poked him to let go.

In no time at all the five of them were headed toward the front door. I barely had time to make it to my room.

"Didja bring me something, Meemee?" Thomas squealed loudly as they came inside. "What d'ja bring me?"

"Here, Meemee. Sit here!" urged Lydia.

I rolled my eyes again. Meemee. Great name. I guess that made her my stepmeemee.

"Charles!" called my mother from the bottom of the stairs. "Charles, come down here! We have company!"

Darn! I knew she'd be calling for me! At our house, my mother treats every person who walks through the front door like royalty or something. Once she made a meat loaf sandwich for a guy selling spot remover.

I started to get dressed. Once I was safely in my clothes, maybe I could sneak onto the roof, lower myself onto the fence, and take off for Martin's house.

"Charles!" demanded my mother again. This time she was at the bottom of the stairs. "Come on down here! See who it is!"

I sighed and slowly sat down on the edge of my bed. There was no use trying to escape. Mom was being too persistent. Soon she'd be coming up to get me.

I still don't know what the big deal was. It wasn't like I was a part of the Russo family or anything. Not a *real* part, related by blood and everything.

I'll never forget when I walked into the living room that morning. Thomas jumped off the couch and started pointing at Mrs. Russo like this was the best thing that had ever happened to him.

"Look! Look! Surprise!" he squeaked. "It's my meemee! It's my meemee!"

You could tell Ben's mother really loved the attention. She was beaming from ear to ear.

"Why, there he is," she exclaimed pleasantly as she held out her hand to me. "How are you, Chuck?"

Chuck. I'm not kidding. She called me Chuck.

Thomas started to laugh. "Chuck? That's not Chuck, you silly. That's Charrulls! He lives with us now."

I turned toward Thomas and frowned. "You live with *me*, you mean," I corrected.

Mrs. Russo wasn't paying attention. Instead, she eyed me suspiciously. Then she turned to Ben.

"Don't they call him Chuck?" she inquired, as if I wasn't even in the room. "I could have sworn at the wedding they called him—"

"No. They don't call me Chuck," I interrupted. "I'm positive."

Ben caught my eye and winked. He was trying to make me feel better, but in my mood it didn't help.

After that, I sat down and listened while the rest of them talked over old times. As it turned out, Ben's mother was famous for popping in on them like that.

" 'Member last year when you surprised Lydia and me and took us to the beach for the weekend, Meemee?" Thomas reminded her happily. "That was fun, wasn't it? 'Member how you let me eat a banana split for dinner and then I got a hot fudge sundae for dessert?"

Suddenly he made a face. " 'Member how my stomach got upset and I spit up the cherry?"

(108)

"Oh, sick, Thomas!" exclaimed Lydia. "Gross. Why'd you have to remind us?"

Thomas started laughing. " 'Member that, Charrulls? That was funny, wasn't it?"

Before I could answer, he shook his head and corrected himself. "Whoops. Forgot. We didn't even know you then."

Mrs. Russo hit herself in the head and grinned. "I guess poor old Meemee doesn't even know him now."

Everyone laughed but me. Even my mother. Like not knowing my name had been the joke of the century.

"Are you gonna stay overnight, Meemee?" Thomas begged, folding his hands together like he was praying. "Please, please, please."

"Of *course* she's going to stay," insisted my mother. "We wouldn't have it any other way."

Mrs. Russo hesitated. "Oh, I don't know. I hadn't really planned on—"

"There's plenty of room for you, Mother," interrupted Ben. "Plenty of room."

I felt myself starting to frown. What room was he talking about? If there was so darned much room, why was I sharing mine?

"I know! I know!" squealed Thomas. "You can stay in my room with me! Right, Dad? Right, Mom?"

I bristled. He called her that name again.

"Hey! I got an idea! Meemee can sleep in Charrulls's bed! It'd be just like at the beach when I slept on that little cot in your room, Meemee!"

Suddenly all eyes turned toward me. I'm not kidding. It's like I was the North Pole and all the eyeballs in the room were magnets. My mother's eyebrows were raised like she was honestly wondering if this would be all right with me.

"I'm sure Charlie won't mind sleeping on the couch for a couple of nights," she said matter-of-factly. "That'd be okay with you, wouldn't it, honey?"

That was it. That was the last straw. Something inside me snapped. And when it did, words came spilling out of my mouth. Words I hadn't even had time to think about.

"Yeah, sure, that'd be perfect! Mrs. Russo can have my bed. Geez, what do I need a bed for? I hardly even have a room anymore."

I stood up and started to leave. "Hey! I've got an idea. I'll sleep under a rock in the back yard. Then I won't be in anyone's way at all. It'll almost be like I don't even exist."

As I started to turn the corner I suddenly stopped and looked back. This time I stared straight at my mom.

"By the way, Mother, I've got some memories,

too, you know. Like remember when we were a
real family—you and Dad and me?"

My eyes darted to Mrs. Russo, then back again.
"We used to go to the beach, too. We went there
a lot. And Dad and I would ride the waves and
have these contests to see who could go the
farthest. He always let me win. I didn't know it
then, but I do now.

"And sometimes Grandma and Granddad
would drive down to the beach and see us for the
weekend. And we'd have picnics in the sand and
Grandma and I would look for shells.

"And they'd come for Thanksgiving, too. We
were just like the families you'd see on those
Butterball commercials. Granddad would carve
the turkey and say this grace he made up about
how lucky we all were to have each other.
Remember that, Mom?"

My voice quieted to a whisper.

"Lucky me."

(ten)

I COULDN'T get out of there fast enough. I slammed the front door. I don't usually explode like that in front of strangers. Normally I save the worst behavior for those I love.

I headed for the park. Or maybe I should say the tree. The same tree where Mom and I had our last picnic and she told me nothing would ever come between us.

When I got about a block away, I started to run. I don't know why I felt in such a hurry to get there. I needed to think things over. But let's face it, all the thinking in the world wasn't going to change anything. It wouldn't solve my problems with Thomas or Lydia. It wouldn't even make Ben and me best friends. Thinking doesn't work miracles. Not even when you end with amen.

As I hurried down the park's sidewalk I couldn't help but notice how many people there were around. It kind of took me by surprise, since I don't usually go to the park on Sundays. But when I finally rounded the corner of the boys' bathroom and spotted the tree, I stopped dead in my tracks. I could hardly believe what I saw. It was covered with kids! Strange little kids were hanging all over its branches!

Hey! I wanted to scream. Get down from there! Out of the tree, you jerks! It's mine!

I didn't, though. It wouldn't have done any good. Two of the little kids had spiked hair and were wearing black rock concert T-shirts. Kids like that don't listen to you unless you have a weapon.

Instead of yelling, I just stood there and watched my tree being overrun. Then I said a cuss word and left.

I started to walk. There was nowhere to go. I called my dad from Circle K. He wasn't home.

After I hung up, I tried Martin's. He was at a soccer game. I didn't call anyone else. I have other friends, but not the kind I needed.

I walked as slowly as I could—scuffing my feet—on my way to nowhere in particular. Like the homeless men you see walking on the street sometimes. I know I was overdoing it on the self-pity, but I couldn't help it. It's a wonder I didn't start collecting aluminum cans.

Walking is boring. Putting one foot in front of the other—that's all it is. My grandfather says that walking puts you in touch with nature. But to me, touching nature isn't that big of a thrill.

Finally my feet started aching and my stomach began to growl. There was no place to go except home. I guess I could have headed downtown to the homeless shelter, but I didn't have the guts. Besides, I have a feeling the homeless shelter is serious business. I don't think they give you a free meal just because your stepmeemee called you Chuck.

When I turned down my block, the first thing I noticed was that the gas guzzler was gone. So far it was the only high point of my day. I didn't know where she went, but I hoped she wouldn't come back.

I also noticed that Ben's truck wasn't there. I couldn't believe it. It was almost too good to be true.

I snuck up to the house and opened the front

door as quietly as I could. Once I was inside I stopped in the hallway to listen for voices.

Please, God, please, I prayed. Just let me get upstairs with no one seeing me. Amen.

The house was silent.

I looked up and whispered, "Thank you." I always look up when I pray. It's a habit from when I was a little kid. MaryAnn Brady told me that God lived on the ceiling.

Making a dash for the dining room, I grabbed two bananas from the bowl on the table. Then I ran to my room and closed the door behind me. Without wasting one more second I opened my window and climbed out onto the roof.

I stood there a minute and breathed in the cool air. I could already feel myself start to calm down.

I climbed higher and settled in my usual spot next to the chimney. I ate the bananas. Then I leaned back and felt the warm sun on my face. I closed my eyes and listened to myself breathing. That's how quiet it was up there.

My nose was making a little whistling noise. In and out . . . in and out . . . in and out . . .

Listening to your own breathing can almost put you to sleep. I guess it's just the rhythm of it or something. In and out . . . in and out . . . slow and steady . . . in and out . . .

Suddenly I felt myself tense up all over again. I covered my ears, but there was no sense pretending I hadn't heard it. Out front, Ben's truck had just pulled into the driveway.

Car doors opened and closed. Thomas's screechy little voice filled the air as he ran for the front door.

"Hey, Mom. I'm gonna see if Charrulls is . . ."

Even though the rest of the sentence was finished in the house, I knew what it was.

". . . home yet," I whispered, feeling sick.

Closing my eyes, I could picture Thomas frantically dashing around trying to find me. In my mind I could almost see where he was in the house.

The living room . . . the kitchen . . . flying down the hall to the stairs . . . taking them two by two . . . now rushing into the bedroom . . . looking around . . . giving the globe a spin . . . looking around some more. Aha! The opened window!

Slowly I began counting to five. I was only on four when Thomas leaned his big head out the window.

"Charrulls!" he exclaimed like he had just

made an important discovery. "There you are!"

He waved. I didn't wave back.

His leg came next. Then his other leg.

"Hey, Charrulls! Look at me!"

The loudness of his own voice seemed to throw him slightly off balance.

"Whoops," he said, holding out his arms to steady himself. He was really shaky. Like he was on a tightrope instead of an entire roof.

"Whoa, it's scary up here, huh, Charrulls?"

"Go back inside, Thomas," I told him. "Please. I just want to sit out here by myself for a while."

He acted like he didn't even hear me. Shaky and stiff-legged, he started inching his way toward me.

"Thomas. Go back inside," I repeated. "I *mean* it."

He hunched over to help balance himself against the steepness of the roof and kept coming. He couldn't seem to talk and walk at the same time.

"God, Thomas!" I finally yelled this time. "Why can't you just leave me alone? Why can't you *ever* just leave me alone?"

Finally, just inches from my foot, he stopped and looked up. His face was frozen in a tense, unnatural grin. There were drops of sweat on his top lip.

Slowly, almost in slow motion, he straightened up. "You shouldn't say God, Charrulls," he said quietly.

Then, still trembling, he studied the distance between us and inched one more step closer. I was just about to yell at him again when suddenly—with no warning at all—he lunged forward and grabbed for my foot.

"No!" I said as his hands reached for my ankle. I pulled my foot away. It was automatic. I didn't even think about it. I just saw him start to grab me and I pulled away.

Thomas fell.

It happened so fast I don't even remember much about it. Or maybe I just don't want to. That happens sometimes. You forget what you don't want to remember.

All I know is that the roof was steep and Thomas couldn't catch himself. And he slipped and rolled toward the edge. And then he was gone. Just like that. He fell.

I heard him hit the ground. I don't want to talk about it, but I heard that noise.

Sometimes when emergencies happen you freeze. You want to help, but you can't. Your brain won't tell you what to do. I saw a dog get hit by a car once. I couldn't even scream.

But this time was different. As soon as I saw

what was happening I slid to the window as fast as I could and pulled myself inside.

"Mom! Ben! Quick! It's Thomas!" I shrieked as loudly as I could. But outside Thomas had already started screaming. And my mother and Ben were racing out the back door to see what had happened.

I should have gone too. I know I should have. But for some reason I just couldn't bring myself to go down there.

Instead, I began frantically pacing back and forth on my floor. "At least he's yelling," I told myself. "At least he's not . . . well, *quiet*. Quiet is bad. Loud is good. Yelling is loud. Yelling is good. . . ."

I just kept babbling on and on like that. I couldn't stop. If I stopped, I might start to think. And if I started to think . . . well, I just didn't want to, that's all.

Suddenly downstairs there was a lot of commotion. Lydia came through the front door just as Mom and Ben were helping Thomas out to the car. Their voices mixed together in loud and confused conversation.

"Hey, what happened? Why's Thomas crying?"

"Here, son, here's a tissue. Hold his arm, Janet."

"Quick, Lydia. Open the front door."

"Somebody tell me what happened!"

"He fell. We're taking him to the emergency room. Are you doing okay, son? Here, wipe your nose. You okay?"

They whisked him out the front door. A second later Ben's truck pulled away. I ran to the end of the hall in time to see it turn the corner.

"Oh God, oh God, oh God . . ."

It's all I could say. It wasn't praying, exactly. But it wasn't cussing either.

"Oh God, oh God, oh God . . ."

I tiptoed back to my room. I got in bed and covered up with my bedspread. A second later I got out again. I paced a few more steps, sat down, sat back up, lay down, stood up, and finally buried my head in the pillow.

He's okay. Yeah, sure he is. No one yells that loud if they're not okay. It was just a little tumble, that's all. A little tumble off the roof. He landed on the grass, right? Grass is soft, right?

Tears filled my eyes. I hadn't meant to hurt him. Why would I want to hurt him? Just because I was upset? That didn't mean anything. Just because I was upset didn't mean I'd hurt him.

It was an accident. Yeah, of course it was. I'm positive. I never would have made him fall on purpose. I don't care if no one believes me, either. I wouldn't have done a thing like that. If I'd known Thomas was going to fall, I never would have pulled away from him the way I did. Honest to God. I wouldn't have.

I wiped my eyes and took a deep breath.

"Just let him be okay. Come on, God. He's only five. Just make him all right."

(eleven)

TWO HOURS. That's how long they were gone. Two hours that seemed more like ten.

As soon as I heard them pull into the driveway I raced downstairs. Lydia was just about to open the door. She looked surprised to see me.

"Where'd you come from?"

I strained to see outside. Thomas was walking up the porch steps with my mother and Ben. His arm was in a sling. Other than that, he seemed to be okay.

I raised my eyes toward the ceiling and said, "Thank you."

Lydia looked at me funny and said, "You're welcome."

After the three of them came inside, things got more confused than ever.

"What did you break, Thomas?" Lydia wanted to know. "What's wrong with your arm?"

Before he could answer, my mother looked at me and frowned. "Where have you been?" she demanded. "We were worried sick about you."

Anxiously Lydia pulled at the rubber band in her hair. "Will someone please tell me what he broke?"

"We didn't know where you were or who you were with or when you were coming home. You know better than to go storming off like that. You know how worried I get."

Lydia was about to explode.

"Collarbone," said Ben, finally answering her.

"Collarbone," echoed Thomas. "It doesn't hurt anymore. I woulda hada cast only they don't put a cast on collarbones. Right, Dad? I just get to have a swing."

"Sling," corrected Ben.

"Next time you pull a stunt like that you're going to be punished," continued my mother, waving her finger in my face.

Lydia still seemed frustrated. "How, though? How did he break it? You can't break your collarbone by just falling over in the grass."

Just for a split second Thomas looked at me. Then he quickly looked away.

"Can too," he said quietly.

Lydia's expression grew angry.

"No, you can't, Thomas!"

"Can too, can too," he repeated just as calmly.

Lydia threw her hands in the air and left the room in a huff.

Ben shook his head. "Didn't take long to get back to normal, did it?"

My mother was still glaring at me. "You and I aren't done yet, bucko," she said. I'm serious. She actually called me bucko.

Ben took her arm and pulled her toward the kitchen. "We'll finish this discussion at dinner," she called, still waving her finger.

I just sighed.

Thomas sat down on the couch. He didn't turn on the television. He just started staring at his sling.

It made me feel sick inside.

I sat down next to him.

"I'm sorry, Thomas," I said softly. "I'm *really* sorry. I never meant for this to happen. It was an accident."

Thomas raised his head. He wasn't smiling exactly, but he didn't look mad, either.

He motioned for me to come closer. Like he had a secret or something.

Careful not to touch his sling, I leaned over next to him.

"I didn't tell, Charrulls," he whispered in my ear.

Puzzled, I raised my eyebrows.

"About what happened on the roof," he explained. "I didn't tattle like I did before."

Even then I didn't fully understand.

Thomas took an exasperated breath. " 'Member how you got mad at me when I told them that you said there was a hand in the closet? Well, this time I didn't tell them what happened. I didn't tattle about anything."

Suddenly I felt even worse than before. How could he have remembered that? How could it have been so important to him?

I didn't know what to say. I just sat there watching Thomas's face grow even more serious. Then, after what seemed to be the longest he had ever been quiet, he finally looked up at me and whispered, "Now you like me. Right, Charrulls?"

GUILT. That's one word I don't have to bother looking up in the dictionary. Everyone knows what guilt means. Guilt is the way you punish yourself when there's no one else to do it for you.

Guilt is a little voice inside your head that screams, "You should be ashamed of yourself!" And even though it's a silent voice, your whole body hears it. And it makes your shoulders slump over a little bit. And sometimes your chin drops down to your chest. And your feet drag when they walk.

That's what guilt does to me, anyway. I'm not kidding. When I finally left Thomas that afternoon, my head and shoulders felt so heavy I wasn't sure I could even get them upstairs.

Now you like me. Right, Charrulls?

I couldn't get it out of my mind. All the way up the steps it kept echoing around in my brain.

You ought to be ashamed of yourself! screamed the silent voice in between echoes. *Poor Thomas. Poor little Thomas.*

When I got to my room I didn't go inside. My feet kept right on going, straight down the hall to the attic door. I can't explain why. They just took me there.

I put my hands over my ears to try to shut out the voice. It wasn't any use, though. When the voice is inside, covering your ears just traps it.

I pulled on the light at the bottom of the staircase and carefully began edging my way around the stack of boxes piled high on the steps. It was dark at the top. There's another light I could have pulled on, but I didn't. Just the mood I was in, I guess. Besides, I know my way around the attic by heart. I know exactly where the pictures are. Even if it was pitch black, I could still find them.

The cardboard box was right where I left it. I picked it up and set it down under the small window in the corner. The fading light coming in was dim and hazy, but there was still enough to see.

I lifted the top and looked at the first photograph. It was the one of me and Dad and the new sandbox he built. I was wearing baggy overalls and holding a hoe. I was practicing to be a farmer.

Tears started to fill my eyes. I didn't want them to. But I guess they'd been building up for quite a while. A second later I started to sniff. That did it. Once the sniffing starts, I'm a goner.

I buried my face in the sleeve of my sweatshirt. Then it all sort of came pouring out at once. I started sobbing and I couldn't stop.

I tried to keep the noise down, but it wasn't easy. Sobbing is like an explosion. All of your emotions erupt like a volcano and everything on your face starts running all at once. The first couple of minutes are the noisiest. But even after that, stuff keeps running. It's a lot to ask a sweatshirt to sop up, if you want to know the truth.

"You okay?"

The voice came out of nowhere. It took me by surprise. Startled, I looked up.

It was Ben! Oh, geez, not now! How had he gotten up the stairs without me hearing?

Instinctively I ducked back into the safety of my soggy sweatshirt. Crying isn't something that I like to do in front of people; I don't care how normal it's supposed to be.

Ben started coming closer. As I heard his footsteps I drew my arms tighter around my hidden face. Somehow I forced myself to stop the tears.

He stood there a moment before sitting down next to me. When he did, our arms touched.

I pulled away.

I was still making quiet snuffling noises by then, but I was pretty much under control. I kept my head down, though. I felt uncomfortable as anything.

Nervously I shifted my feet. What should I do? What should I say? Did he know? Should I confess?

I rolled my eyes. Confess? Yeah, sure . . . right, Charlie.

Oh, by the way, Ben, I made Thomas fall off the

roof and break his collarbone. He's keeping it a secret so I'll like him.

I felt more tears well up in my eyes. I was going to start crying again. I just couldn't find a way out.

Without saying a word, Ben reached out for me. I felt his arm around me, and I buried my face in his shoulder. I didn't even think about it.

We stayed like that until the crying stopped again. It wasn't the noisy kind this time. Just the quiet, muffled sniffling you do when you're finishing up.

Through it all, Ben didn't say a word. Except for my sniffling and a little gulping, the two of us remained silent. The silence wasn't awkward, though. Not like the strained silences we'd had on our trip to Lake Murky.

When I was finished, I lifted my face off his shoulder and wiped my eyes. Ben gave me one last pat and removed his arm. No sense overdoing the hugging stuff. Not when neither one of us was used to it.

I couldn't think of anything to say. I guess Ben couldn't either. The awkwardness was coming between us again. You could almost feel it start to separate us.

I couldn't stand it this time. Maybe it was the guilt. Or maybe I just felt closer to Ben than I had before.

"Thomas fell off the roof," I blurted out suddenly. "I was out there and he reached for me and I pulled away and he fell."

I turned and looked him in the eye. "He did, Ben. I didn't push him. I thought maybe I did at first, but I didn't. I wouldn't have done that. I know I wouldn't have."

Ben took his hand and brushed the hair back from my forehead. Then he looked at me and slowly nodded.

I waited for more, but it never came. He believed me, though. I could see in his eyes that he believed me.

We sat there another couple of minutes before Ben suddenly reached across my lap and picked up the photo of Dad and me and the sandbox. It was lying face down next to my leg. He turned it over and smiled.

The smile turned into a chuckle.

"Great picture," he said, laughing softly. "That hoe was twice as big as you were."

I sniffed and nodded.

He reached out and pulled the cardboard box of photos closer.

"Would you mind if I looked through the rest of these?" he asked, already digging into the carton.

I felt myself tensing up again. There was something about Ben looking into my box of pictures that felt wrong. I mean, the sandbox picture wasn't really that personal. But to look through the whole box—I don't know—it was almost like he was invading my family's privacy or something.

I was still thinking it over when I heard Ben take a deep breath.

"Susan used to take a lot of pictures," he said almost in a whisper.

It was the first time he'd ever mentioned his wife's name. Susan.

Ben didn't get weepy or anything. He just stared into space a second and then quickly reached into the box again. How could I say no after that?

The next picture was the most recent one that Mom and Dad and I had taken together. It was taken in a studio, the kind where the photographer gives you a choice of fake backgrounds to stand in front of.

I cleared my throat. "Those aren't really the Alps," I told Ben. "It's just a picture of Alps."

I wasn't planning to explain every photograph. I just didn't want him asking me a bunch of questions about Switzerland, that's all.

The next picture was taken during one of our first family vacations.

Ben raised his eyebrows. "Disney World?"

"Land," I corrected.

He pointed at me in the picture and smiled. "Thomas has one of those Donald Duck hats."

My face turned red. I've never really forgiven my parents for buying me that hat. I know I begged, but they should have been stronger.

After another second or two, Ben dug deeper into the carton. I swallowed hard. Now we were getting to the personal stuff. My heart began to beat faster. I was almost positive which picture was next.

Maybe I should have warned Ben it was coming.

"Their wedding picture," I blurted loudly.

Ben was surprised. You could see it in his eyes. The glass was smudged and dirty with finger-prints from all the times I'd held it. But he lowered it to his lap and stared through the smudges.

It was one of those pictures that you imagine seeing at the end of fairy tales. My mother was in this beautiful white gown and Dad was wearing one of those suits with a sash around the middle. They were standing in front of the altar in the church, kissing.

See? I wanted to yell. They really *did* love each other once!

I didn't, though. I just sat there with my heart still pounding like crazy while Ben stared down at the picture. It took him a long time, too. I didn't have a watch or anything, but it was definitely a while.

Finally he took a big deep breath and turned to me. Then he smiled this really sad smile.

"It's really been hard on you, hasn't it?" he asked me softly.

I didn't answer.

"I'm sorry," he whispered. "I wish I could have made things easier for you. I just didn't know how."

He put his arm around my shoulders again and held me.

I didn't pull away.

(twelve)

THOMAS GOT to take his sling off a few weeks ago. You can tell that he misses the attention it brought him. The other day he made a sling out of an old towel and wore it to dinner. He asked Lydia to cut his meat loaf. Ben told him to go upstairs until he could act normal.

I guess you could say the two of us are making progress. Thomas and me, I mean. The last time Martin came over to play Monopoly, he started making the top hat and the iron dance with each other.

"Stop it, Thomas," I ordered.

He ignored me.

"I mean it. Put them down."

He continued to dance them around the board. I had no choice.

"Okay, Thomas. That's it. If you don't stop, I'm going to make the hand come out of the closet and kill you."

Thomas isn't as worried about the hand as he used to be. He put his mouth on his arm and started making bathroom noises. He seemed to think this was really hilarious. He was still laughing when I dragged him into the hall and locked him out of the room.

Martin was very impressed. He said as soon as we get a little more violent, we'll be practically normal.

I don't want to make everything sound okay, because it's not. This isn't one of those "they lived happily ever after" endings. I don't believe in those anymore.

Lydia still hogs the phone like crazy. She sits there for hours saying absolutely nothing of interest. I'm serious. I've had better conversations with a Mattel SEE 'N SAY.

Also, she still locks herself in the bathroom. These days I'm not as nice about it as I used to be. If I want to get in there, I just pound on the door and start screaming, "I gotta go! I gotta go!" When it comes to going to the bathroom, I have no pride.

The two of us don't fight exactly. Mostly we just make fun of each other. Like the other night when I took off my tennis shoes, she held her nose.

"P.U.! What died?"

"Whoops, sorry," I apologized. "I almost forgot. Big noses are more sensitive than normal ones."

"There's nothing wrong with my nose," she snapped defensively.

"I didn't say there was, Lydia. Noses like yours come in very handy. If we ever have a fire, you can spray it out."

"Daaa-aad!" she screamed.

When Lydia tattles, she makes *dad* into two syllables.

Speaking of dads, mine took me to the zoo for the hundredth time last weekend. We don't look at the animals anymore. Mostly we just have a picnic lunch and talk and stuff.

My father told me that he'd noticed a difference in me lately.

"You don't seem to be as angry as you used to be," he commented. "What d'you think? You think that maybe you're finally starting to adjust to your new situation?"

"No!" I retorted quickly. "I'm not adjusting.

Just because I'm not sulking all the time doesn't mean I'm adjusting."

I hate it when parents think you're adjusting. It takes the guilt off of them or something.

I'll tell you one person who's finally started to change, though, and that's my mother. I'm serious. She's finally beginning to treat Thomas the way she should have treated him all along. The other day he called her a "giant poopy" and she marched him right up to our room and made him stay there all day.

Thomas still wasn't speaking to her at dinner. Even though we were having hamburgers, he refused to eat.

I could hardly keep from laughing. It was great seeing someone else in trouble for a change. Just to be annoying, I stuffed a giant bite of cheeseburger into my mouth and grinned at Thomas with my mouth opened. Ben said for me to get down from the table until I could eat like a human being.

Speaking of Thomas, he turned six last week. I gave him my globe. No big deal. I just slapped on a bow and handed it to him during the ice cream and cake.

His eyes lit up like you wouldn't believe. "Mine? Is this for me? I get to have your world?"

I just shrugged. It's not like it cost me anything. And besides, I already know what the world looks like. It's round and it's bumpy and it spins.

But mostly it changes. Volcanoes blow up and the seasons go from winter to summer and every day turns into night. And people get divorced and then they get married again and the next thing you know, you're sharing your bedroom. And sometimes you're angry and sometimes you're sad, and sometimes you're so confused, you don't know what you are.

And they say that time fixes everything, but it doesn't. Not everything. Time can't change what's already happened. It can only help you accept it a little easier, that's all.

And even if some of the anger starts to go away after a while, you don't have to run around telling your parents how much better you're feeling.

And you don't have to eat fiber cereal either.

Oh, yeah, and you don't have to keep your memories in a box in the attic. You can bring them down and put them on your dresser if you want to.

You can.

Ben helped.